marshall mcluhan

essays

media

research

technology, art, communication

edited with
commentary

michel

a. moos

G+B
ARTS
INTERNATIONAL

Australia · Canada · China · France · Germany · India · Japan · Luxembourg · Malaysia
The Netherlands · Russia · Singapore · Switzerland · Thailand · United Kingdom

Amsteldijk 166
1st Floor
1079 LH Amsterdam
The Netherlands

British Library Cataloguing in Publication Data

McLuhan, Marshall, 1911–1980
    Media research : technology, art, communication.
    (Critical voices in art, theory and culture)
    1. Mass media and technology   2. Mass media and culture
    I. Title   II. Moos, Michel A.
    302. 2'34

ISBN 90-5701-091-7

Grateful acknowledgment is made to Matie Molinaro, Corinne McLuhan and the Marshall McLuhan Estate for permission to publish the work of Marshall McLuhan included in this volume. I would like here to express my gratitude to Saul Ostrow, T. C. McLuhan and David Moos for invaluable advice and encouragement, as well as to Alfred van der Marck and Liza Rudneva for their editorial support and expertise, and to my wife Lane for both the message and the medium generously tendered.

Michel A. Moos

To Walter and Martha

CONTENTS

INTRODUCTION TO THE SERIES

*C*ritical Voices in Art, Theory and Culture is a response to the changing perspectives that have resulted from the continuing application of structural and poststructural methodologies and interpretations to the cultural sphere. From the ongoing processes of deconstruction and reorganization of the traditional canon, new forms of speculative, intellectual inquiry and academic practices have emerged which are premised on the realization that insights into differing aspects of the disciplines that make up this realm are best provided by an interdisciplinary approach that follows a discursive rather than a dialectic model.

In recognition of these changes, and of the view that the histories and practices that form our present circumstances are in turn transformed by the social, economic, and political requirements of our lives, this series will publish not only those authors who already are prominent in their field, or those who are now emerging—but also those writers who had previously been acknowledged, then passed over, only now to become relevant once more. This multigenerational approach will give many writers an opportunity to analyze and reevaluate the position of those thinkers who have influenced their own practices, or to present responses to the themes and writings that are significant to their own research.

In emphasizing dialogue, self-reflective critiques, and exegesis, the *Critical Voices* series not only acknowledges the deterritorialized nature of our present intellectual environment, but also extends the challenge to the traditional supremacy of the authorial voice by literally relocating it within a discursive network. This approach to texts breaks with the current practice of speaking of multiplicity, while continuing to construct a singularly linear vision of discourse that retains the characteristics of dialectics. In an age when subjects are conceived of as acting upon one another, each within the context of its own history and without contradiction, the ideal of a totalizing system does not seem to suffice. I have come to realize that the near collapse of the endeavor to produce homogeneous terms, practices, and histories—once thought to be an essential aspect of defining the practices of art, theory, and culture—reopened each of these subjects to new interpretations and methods.

My intent as editor of *Critical Voices in Art, Theory and Culture* is to make available to our readers heterogeneous texts that provide a view that looks ahead to new and differing approaches, and back toward those views that make the dialogues and debates developing within the areas of cultural studies, art history, and critical theory possible and necessary. In this manner we hope to contribute to the expanding map not only of the borderlands of modernism, but also of those newly opened territories now identified with postmodernism.

Saul Ostrow

Marshall McLuhan: The Messenger's Medium

*G*uy Debord proposes that the Society of the Spectacle begins in 1937. Though he does not register any specific event, it is worth noting this is the year that commercial television puts in its first appearance and with it the promise of endless access to entertainment and information. Given the central role the mass media and culture play in his vision of late capitalist society, it should come as no surprise that he has something to say about Herbert Marshall McLuhan. The *context* of these remarks is unexpected; they come amid observations on the "permanent self-denial that is the price an individual pays for the tiniest bit of social status." On pp. 33–34 of "Comments on the Society of the Spectacle," Debord writes: "... MacLuhan [*sic*] himself, the spectacle's first apologist, who seemed to be the most convinced imbecile of the century, changed his mind when he finally discovered in 1976 that the pressure of the mass media leads to irrationality and that it was becoming urgent to modify their usage."

To the Situationists, the fact that the "sage of Toronto" had spent several decades marveling at the numerous freedoms that were supposed to be constantly and effortlessly accessible to all because telecommunications was creating a "global village" is presented as proof of McLuhan's feeblemindedness. Taking the term "global village" literally, Debord reminds us that "Villages, unlike towns, have always been ruled by conformism, isolation, petty surveillance, boredom and repetitious, malicious gossip. . . ." Which from Debord's perspective is "precise enough description of the global spectacle's vulgarity, in which it has become impossible to distinguish the Grimaldi–Monaco or Bourbon–Franco dynasties from those that succeeded the Stuarts." (I assume this reference is Debord's obtuse way of identifying that one of the effects of this globalization is that it brings with it historical unconsciousness and indeterminancy.)

Because McLuhan's optimism waned and his changed views no longer served the cause of the mass marketing of electronic media, Debord observes that his ungrateful disciples are now trying to make people forget him, "hoping to establish their own careers in media celebrating all these new freedoms to 'choose' at random from ephemera." Debord observes that "they no doubt will retract their claims even faster than the man who inspired them." This disdain for McLuhan's early confidence and the lateness of his acknowledgment of the negative effects of the new electronic media did not prevent the Situationists from incorporating McLuhan's insights into their critique of late "capital."

While left-wing intellectuals heaped criticism on McLuhan for his humanism and others hotly debated the merits of his views, his ability to sum up complex ideas in sound bytes—Gutenberg galaxy, media hot and media cool, the medium is the message—made him a celebrity. His ideas were discussed in the popular press (he was interviewed for *Playboy* magazine) and he even appeared on late-night talk shows. McLuhan had achieved this status by bringing to our attention, along with the likes of Andy Warhol and Timothy Leary, the effect mass media were having on the society that was tuning into it. At the height of this notoriety, Woody Allen, in the film *Annie Hall* brings him out from behind a potted palm to explain his theories to a boorish upper-westside New York pseudointellectual type. This appearance in a mainstream film, even if only as an inside joke, demonstrates that this Canadian professor of literature had escaped the confines of academia and had gained mass audience name recognition.

Beyond his Pop-icon status, McLuhan, armed with a humanist ideology, engaged his subject using a discursive (interpretive) methodology rather than the standard Marxist-influenced critique of the Frankfurt School. Though optimistic about the potential power of the new media, McLuhan did not like playing the prophet; instead he was describing the process of change that was already under way. In the late 1950s and early 1960s this entailed both creating and shattering the utopian dream of a "global village" of common knowledge, culture and expectations. This "village" was to be the result of the fact that our relationship to time and space was being altered by the way electronic media were making every event, everywhere immediately accessible.

The problem was the images that had the greatest effects on the public of the 1960s were those of brutality and deception, be they police attacks on civil rights demonstrators or the rising casualty count from the expanding war in Vietnam. The fact that they were intercut with commercials and "sit-coms" did not go unnoticed. These intrusive images made us aware that the new mythology of the liberating effect of the free flow of information had its flip side— it made us all witnesses and accomplices. While capable at first of outraging and then through repetition pacifying us, the new televisual medium also supplied diversion. It filled our leisure time, whet our appetites with fantasies and supplied an endless parade of new objects of desire. In the comfort of our own homes, the alternating currents of "hot images and cool media" made us ever more susceptible to the subversive message of the medium itself: "Sit back, we will bring it all to you."

Electronic media had not only changed our world view by speeding up information's dissemination and retrieval, but its binary and immaterial nature constituted a silent revolution. The slogan "the medium is the message" became the central and most popular theme of McLuhan's analysis. By examining everything from sixteenth-century literature to twentieth-century business practices McLuhan sought to expose the effect of the forces hidden deep within telecommunication and digital technologies. From his point of view technology was an extension of our senses; so in his representation of *electric* man, the dynamic of electronic media is neither neutral nor mechanical but neural. Throughout, he emphasizes that electronic media collapse time and space, creating a *hyperreal*—a here and now in which the ear becomes the eye's equal, and the audile-tactile empire of our senses is reinvigorated.

As the chaotic 1960s gave way to the drab and sluggish 1990s, the conscious adjustment of reality brought on by the shift from a mechanical to an electronic age gave way to unconscious absorption. Optimism waned; the new world of the 1970s was harsher than that of the exuberant and savage days of cultural and social revolution. As attentions wandered, the amplified syncopation of rock 'n roll gave way to disco's synthesized, monotonous beat and what had only a few years before seemed a marvel was now taken for granted. Things had become automated, faster and miniaturized; innovations and new products had come to be expected. Ironically, despite an awareness that television was being used to manipulate and manage our consciousness, electronic media worked their spell anyway. For the real effect of the media revolution was that while it distributed data it also consumed it.

Events in the world could not keep up with an ever-expanding demand, so through a process of repetition, variation and recycling, information came to be manufactured and standardized. Andy Warhol knew that the endless appetite of the media would eventually make everyone famous for fifteen minutes. McLuhan had told us, but we hadn't really understood what he meant, when he said that the content of any given medium was what it did to the structure of information. The transparency of electronic media's ideological manipulation and denigration of its audience gave its real effect a certain invulnerability.

By the 1980s McLuhan's fame faded; he was best known as having been a Pop icon, though he did remain a cult figure for a small band of media experts and communications students. Beyond this, there was no longer serious discussion of his ideas. His books slowly went out of print, disappeared from bookstore shelves and found their way instead into secondhand bins. The world sought its explanations in new theories and views, ones that would allow us to orient ourselves and make sense of an environment that promised multiple virtual realities. The postmodern era had emerged.

Paradoxically, in the wake of promotion of the "information highway" and the digital revolution, McLuhan has been brought out from behind a potted palm again. This time, rather than correcting the misunderstanding of a hip upper-westside New York type trying to impress his girlfriend, Pop apologists created digital séances in which virtual McLuhans theorize the Internet as the road to higher consciousness and global community. No place in the reverie of interactive computer-generated virtual reality do we find a warning that "the pressure of the mass media leads to irrationality" nor the fact that it is "urgent to modify their usage." McLuhan has been dubbed spin doctor of the digital revolution, the ghostly booster for virtual communities and the prophet and patron saint of business on the Internet. The most significant consequence of twenty years of neglect is that it allows the myth of the electronic age as one of autonomy, access and decentralization to be foisted, virtually unchecked, on another generation.

Michel Moos is not interested in bemoaning this situation. Instead, while acknowledging the complexity of McLuhan's endeavor to describe technology's effects on all aspects of human activity, Moos finds in McLuhan an oracle of another order. He discovers that the structure of McLuhan's simple and jargon-free writing forms a nascent model of hypertext, in that it abandons linearity for the discursive logic of the data byte. In analyzing the structure of his prose, Moos focuses our attention on an aspect of McLuhan's work that has gone largely unnoticed, the very prose medium by which McLuhan objectified his own thoughts.

McLuhan had recognized that electronic media, by displacing print as the dominant means of distributing information, had diminished the authority of the visual space of the Renaissance, therefore dismantling the visual/literate bias of Western culture that had been reenforced by the advent of printing. Moos' own background in comparative and medieval literature makes him sensitive to the need for language to seek the means to represent its own changing status as well as that of our modes of thought. Read in the context of not only what McLuhan has to say but also how he says it, Moos uncovers an author whose work casts new light on the issues arising out of recent postmodernist practices.

Using the works of such poststructuralists as Michel Foucault, Fredric Jameson, Friedrich Kittler, Donna Haraway, Roland Barthes and the theses on representation of Jean Baudrillard, Paul Virilio and Deleuze and Guattari, Moos illuminates how McLuhan's authorial practices reflect the pressures exerted on written language by the very electronic media that are McLuhan's subject. This perspective forms a feedback loop that has profound theoretical implications beyond those concerning alterations induced by technological change. Using this as his point of entry, Moos connects the content of McLuhan's form to the more compelling questions confronting critical endeavors of the humanities in our post-Modern age. In Moos' opinion, McLuhan serves as a detailed model for a disciplined process of reeducation and training along the interdisciplinary and discursive lines that our age of reproduction, interactivity and digitalization requires. Moos, by rendering an updated account of McLuhan's practice as an author, indicates how his vision and influence extend well beyond both their Pop reception in the 1960s and his consecration in the 1990s.

Saul Ostrow

ESSAYS BY
MARSHALL McLUHAN

*T*he chief purpose of this collection is to situate the work of Marshall McLuhan at the intersection of speculative and cultural formations across a broad range of critical and aesthetic contexts. Spanning twenty years (1953–1973), the ten selections included in this volume comprise seven essays, a book review, a lecture, and an interview. Four of the essays—**Culture Without Literacy** (1953), **Acoustic Space** (1955), **Radio and TV vs. The Abced-Minded** (1955), **Myth and Mass Media** (1959)—date from the fertile period after the publication of McLuhan's first book, *The Mechanical Bride* (1951) but before *The Gutenberg Galaxy* (1962) and *Understanding Media* (1964), during which McLuhan makes his breakthrough, namely: "that we had already passed out of the mechanistic age into the electronic."[1] Here and throughout, McLuhan demonstrates the resourcefulness of a poet and the laconic elegance of a structural engineer's way of thinking to articulate the causes and effects of massive cultural transition. Thus he derives the new *acoustic* space of electronic media directly out of the *light* bulb ("The electric light is pure information. It is a medium without a message"[2]); likewise his economic suggestion in **Myth and Mass Media** that language and mass media be treated covalently as "macromyths" at once releases postmodern thought from the prison-house structural linguistics built when it asserted the centrality of literary structures to the organization of experience—and not the reverse. As is early evidenced in the bold strokes of **Culture Without Literacy** (1953), McLuhan's heuristics grounds a new paradigm of intellection upon hypotheses fully congruent with the observed effects of electromagnetic communication. This is why he cannot be said to borrow from the "sciences," as is now the trend in postmodern theory.

Notes on Burroughs (1964) shows McLuhan already conversant with a cyberspace in which, wittingly or no, bodies function as "hydraulic jacks" cathected into a series of purpose-made "anti-environments" which reprogram the sensory order of the environment itself. The essay **The Relation of Environment to Anti-Environment** (1967) presents revised meditation on the now ubiquitous catchphrase, for as McLuhan reckons, "To say that any technology or extension of man creates a new environment is a much better way of saying that *the medium is the message*. This environment is always 'invisible' and its content is always the old technology."[3] McLuhan continues to set the agenda for our thinking about electronic media because the Socratic directness of his consideration of complex human and social processes is a basis for navigating the perceptual bias of technologically induced habits of mind. That McLuhan was primarily concerned with "training perception and sensibility" is perhaps the most overlooked factor in understanding how his thinking still prominently defines our entry into the Information Age. It is with an eye to the subliminally obvious that **The End of the Work Ethic** (1973) vividly recounts "What Ever Happened to The Great American Job?" well before the pressures of downsizing make themselves known;[4] it is noteworthy as well for the fact that McLuhan delivers the address extempore, it being his custom to "never use a written manuscript for talks." With **Radio and TV vs. The Abced-Minded** (1955) McLuhan not only proves a comprehensive reader of Joyce's *Finnegans Wake*—an accomplishment in itself—but advances the electronic use of language as electrode or resonant pickup for consciously probing the multimedia surround. As he explains in **The Electronic Age—The Age of Implosion** (1962), the population explosion is the implosion of "the models of perception and learning," rendering us all "global villagers" under the imperative of accomodating our perceptions and judgments to the "complex interdependence . . . of an electronically unified world."[5] The new sensitivity developed in adjusting to such exponential involution is what **The Agenbite of Outwit** (1963) refers to, sudden consciousness of an ecological "agon," the crisis of the body in extension now that technology stands revealed as the *outering* of our wits or senses and therefore our selves. In McLuhan's radical, transformative analysis, in his insistence on maximizing "contact with the life of forms,"[6] lies that rare refusal to feign a simplicity that just isn't there; the fatuous reduction his terms continue to undergo indicates the paucity of means that existed before him, as well as the tenacity of investment in past solutions to present problems. Amidst the hype attendant upon the business of communicating, it may be surprising to learn in **The *Hot and Cool* Interview** (1967) that "the communications expert" regards communication itself as an "exceedingly difficult activity . . . actually very rare in human affairs."[7]

It is my view that the body of McLuhan's work, as a concerted effort to map psychic and social shifts in "the geography of perception and feeling,"[8] provides a "road map" of the electronic sensorium or "cybercosm"—as it might be thought: a global mindscape of telempathic potential—in which we live, one which serious critical and artistic ventures increasingly cannot afford to be without. To the extent that conclusions he arrived at not only still hold, but go a long way toward illuminating complexities couched in such notions as the "digital age" and the "information highway," McLuhan's treatment of the "infoscape" that surrounds us as a cacophony of so many "languages" may go far to avert the reductionist thinking and rhetoric of the technocrat. If McLuhan remains not merely relevant but still ahead of much postmodern conception and debate, if the feedback he supplies continues to yield valuable feedforward, it is becoming apparent that this has less to do with the popular interpretation or side effect of his success than with the fact that his training led him to rethink in detail the process of education and learning itself. These essays represent part of a unique and original effort to reconsider cultural practices from the perspective of a new concept of cultural materialism, one that radically redefines postmodern formulations of discourse and the body. At very least, the premise for McLuhan's study of the constructs of interpersonal life can tell us why in the humanities, with the growing evanescence of human interface, we yet remain remedial with respect to our media.

M. A. M.

M Y T H   A N D
M A S S   M E D I A

*W*hen an attempt is made to bring the relatively articulated concept of "myth" into the area of "media"—a concept to which surprisingly little attention has been given in the past—it is necessary to reconsider both "myth" and "media" in order to get at relevant data. For example, English is itself a mass medium, as is any language employed by any society. But the general use of the phrase "mass media" would seem to record an unfavorable valuation of new media, especially since the advent of the telegraph, the telephone, moving pictures, radio, and television. These media have had the same kind of drastic effect on language and culture that print had in Europe in the sixteenth century, or that it is now having in other parts of the world.

It might even be well to avoid so highly charged a phrase as "mass media" until a little more thought can be given to the problem. Languages as human artifacts, collective products of human skill and need, can easily be regarded as "mass media," but many find it difficult to consider the newer media deriving from these languages as new "languages." Writing, in its several modes, can be regarded technologically as the development of new languages. For to translate the audible into the visible by phonetic means is to institute a dynamic process that reshapes every aspect of thought, language, and society. To record the extended operation of such a process in a Gorgon or Cadmus myth is to reduce a complex historical affair to an inclusive timeless image. Can we, perhaps, say that in the case of a single word, myth is present as a single snapshot of a complex process, and that in the case of a narrative myth with its peripety, a complex process is recorded in a single inclusive image? The multilayered montage or "transparency," with its abridgement of logical relationships, is as familiar in the cave painting as in cubism.

Oral cultures are simultaneous in their modes of awareness. Today we come to the oral condition again via the electronic media, which abridge space and time and single-plane relationships, returning us to the confrontation of multiple relationships at the same moment.

If a language contrived and used by many people is a mass medium, any one of our new media is in a sense a new language, a new codification of experience collectively achieved by new work habits and inclusive collective awareness. But when such a new codification has reached the technological stage of communicability and repeatability, has it not, like a spoken tongue, also become a macromyth? How much compression of the elements of a process must occur before one can say that they are certainly in mythic form? Are we inclined to insist that myth be a reduction of collective experience to a visual and classifiable form?

Languages old and new, as macromyths, have that relation to words and word-making that characterizes the fullest scope of myth. The collective skills and experience that constitute both spoken languages and such new languages as movies or radio can also be considered with preliterate myths as static models of the universe. But do they not tend, like languages in general, to be dynamic models of the universe in action? As such, languages old and new would seem to be for participation rather than for contemplation or for reference and classification.

Another way of getting at this aspect of languages as macromyths is to say that the medium is the message. Only incidentally, as it were, is such a medium a specialized means of signifying or of reference. And in the long run, for such media or macromyths as the phonetic alphabet, printing, photography, the movie, the telegraph, the telephone, radio, and television, the social action of these forms is also, in the fullest sense, their message or meaning. A language is, on the one hand, little affected by the use individuals make of it; but, on the other hand, it almost entirely patterns the character of what is thought, felt, or said by those using it. And it can be utterly changed by the intrusion of another language, as speech was changed by writing, and radio by television.

Is, then, what concerns us as "myth" today a photograph or "still" shot of a macromyth in action? As a word uttered is an auditory arrest of mental motion, and the phonetic translation of that sound into visual equivalence is a frozen image of the same, is not myth a means of static abstraction from live process? A kind of myth-making process is often associated with Hollywood and with Madison Avenue advertising agencies. So far as advertisements are concerned, they do, in intention at least, strive to comprise in a single image the total social action or process that is imagined as desirable. That is, an advertisement tries both to inform us about, and also to produce in us by anticipation, all the stages of a metamorphosis, private and social. So that whereas a myth might appear as the record of such extended metamorphosis, an advertisement proceeds by anticipation of change, simultaneously anticipating causes with effects and effects with causes. In myth this fusion and telescoping of phases of process becomes a kind of explanation or mode of intelligibility.

What are the myths by which men have recorded the action of new media on their lives? Is there significance in the fact that the Oedipus myth has so far not been found among the preliterate? Is the action of literacy in the shaping of individualism and nationalism also severe on kinship structures? Is the Gorgon myth an account of the effects of literacy in arresting the modes of knowledge? Certainly the Cadmus myth about letters as the dragon's teeth that sprang up armed men is an image of the dynamics of literacy in creating empires. H. A. Innis in his *Empire and Communications* has given us a full exegesis of the Cadmus myth. But the Gorgon myth is in much greater need of exegesis, since it concerns the role of media in learning and knowing. Today, when by means of a computer it is easy to translate a mere blueprint of an unbuilt plane into a wind-tunnel test flight, we find it natural to take all flat data into the domain of depth interpretation. Electronic culture accepts the simultaneous as a reconquest of auditory space. Since the ear picks up sound from all directions at once, thus creating a spherical field of experience, it is natural that electronically moved information should also assume this spherelike pattern. Since the telegraph, then, the forms of Western culture have been strongly shaped by the spherelike pattern that belongs to a field of awareness in which all the elements are practically simultaneous.

It is this instantaneous character of the information field today, inseparable from electronic media, that confers the formal auditory character on the new culture. That is to say, for example, that the newspaper page, since the introduction of the telegraph, has had a formally auditory character and only incidentally a lineal, literary form. Each item makes its own world, unrelated to any other item save by date line. And the assembly of items constitutes a kind of global image in which there is much overlay and montage but little pictorial space or perspective. For electronically moved information, in being simultaneous, assumes the total-field pattern, as in auditory space. And preliterate societies likewise live largely in the auditory or simultaneous mode with an inclusiveness of awareness that increasingly characterizes our electronic age. The traumatic shock of moving from the segmental, lineal space of literacy into the auditory, unified field of electronic information is quite unlike the reverse process. But today, while we are resuming so many of the preliterate modes of awareness, we can at the same time watch many preliterate cultures beginning their tour through the cultural phases of literacy.

The phonetic alphabet, which permits the translation of the audible into the visible, does so by suppression of meaning in the sounds of the letters. This very abstract technology has made possible a continuous one-way conquest of cultures by the Western world that is far from finished. But it would seem that with the commercial use of the telegraph during more than a century we have become accessible to Eastern art and technology as well as to preliterate and auditory cultures in general. At least, let us be prepared to consider carefully the formally auditory character in the telegraph and in subsequent electronic forms of codifying information. For the formal causes inherent in such media operate on the matter of our senses. The effect of media, like their "message," is really in their form and not in their content. And their formal effect is always subliminal so far as our ideas and concepts are concerned.

It is easy to trace some of the effects of phonetic writing since they are coextensive with the most familiar features of the Western world.

The phonetically written word, itself an abstract image of a spoken word, permits the prolonged analysis of process but does not greatly encourage the application of knowledge to action beyond the verbal sphere. It is not strange, therefore, that the ancient world should have considered applied knowledge under the mode of rhetoric. For writing made it possible to card-catalogue all the individual postures of mind called the "figures" of rhetoric. And these became available to all students as direct means of control over other minds. The oligarchic reign of these figures was swiftly liquidated by printing, a technique that shifted attention from the audience to the mental state of the individual reader.

Writing has given the means of segmenting many phases of knowing and doing. Applied knowledge by the lineal segmentation of outward motion comes with print, which is itself the first mechanization of an ancient handicraft. And whereas writing had fostered the classification of the arts and sciences in depth, print gave access to the arts and sciences at high speed and on one plane at a time. While manuscript culture required gloss and commentary to extract the various levels of meaning it held for the awareness, because of the very slow reading necessary, print is itself commentary or explanation. The form of print is single-leveled. And the print-reader is greatly disposed to feel that he is sharing the movements of another mind. Print drove people like Montaigne to explore the medium as a new art form providing an elaborate means of self-investigation in the act of learning, as well as self-portraiture and self-expression.

By contrast, today we live in a postliterate and electronic world, in which we seek images of collective postures of mind, even when studying the individual. In some respects, myth was the means of access to such collective postures in the past. But our new technology gives us many new means of access to group-dynamic patterns. Behind us are five centuries during which we have had unexampled access to aspects of private consciousness by means of the printed page. But now anthropology and archaeology give us equal ease of access to group postures and patterns of many cultures, including our own.

Electronic tape permits access to the structure and group dynamics of entire languages. My suggestion that we might regard languages on one hand as mass media and on the other as macromyths seems obvious to the point of triteness to the structural linguists to whom I have mentioned these approaches. But it may be useful to point to some of the many nonverbal postures, both individual and public, that accompany changes in the media. That is to say, a new form is usually a cluster of items. For example, in the very first decades of printing at the end of the fifteenth century, people became vividly aware of the camera obscura. The relation of this interest to the new printing process was not noted at the time. Yet printing is itself just such a camera obscura, yielding a private vision of the movements of others. While sitting in the dark, one has in the camera obscura a cinematic presentation of the outside world. And in reading print, the reader acts as a kind of projector of the still shots or printed words, which he can read fast enough to have the feeling of re-creating the movements of another mind. Manuscripts could not be read at a speed sufficient to create the sense of a mind actively engaged in learning and in self-expression. But here, centuries before the movie, is the ultimate magic and myth of the movie in the camera obscura. Perhaps as the camera obscura was the first, the movie is the last phase of print technology.

The movie, which has so little in common with television, may be the last image of the Gutenberg era before it fuses via the telegraph, the telephone, radio, and television, and fades into the new world of auditory space. And as the habits of reading print create intense forms of individualism and nationalism, do not our instantaneous electronic media return us to group dynamics, both in theory and in practice? Is not this shift in media the key to our natural concern with the concept and relevance of myth today?

Printing evoked both individualism and nationalism in the sixteenth century, just as it will do again in India, Africa, China, and Russia. For it demands habits of solitary initiative and attention to exactly repeatable commodities, which are the habits inseparable from industry, and enterprise, production and marketing. Where production precedes literacy, there is no uniform market and no price structure. Industrial production without well-established markets and literacy makes "communism" necessary. Such is the state of our own ignorance of our media that we are surprised to find that radio has very different effects in an oral society than it had in our highly literate culture. In the same way the "nationalism" of an oral world is structured quite differently from the nationalism of a newly literate society. It would appear that to see one's mother tongue dignified with the precise technology of print releases a new vision of unity and power, which remains a subliminal divisive force in the West even today. Unawareness of the effects of our media these past two thousand years and more would seem to be itself an effect of literacy that James Joyce designated as "ab-ced" or absent-mindedness. The sentiment of spatial and territorial nationalism that accompanies literacy is also reinforced by the printing press, which provides not only the sentiment but also the centralized bureaucratic instruments of uniform control over wide territories.

Perhaps we tend to define myth in too literary a way, as something that can be verbalized, narrated, and written down. If we can regard all media as myths and as the prolific source of many subordinate myths, why cannot we spot the mythic aspect of the current hula-hoop activity? Here is a myth we are living. Many people have puzzled over the fact that children refuse to roll these hoops on roads or walks. A mere thirty years ago a hoop was for rolling. Today children reject the lineal use of the hoop in an external space. They use it in a nuclear mode as a means of generating their own space. Here, then, is a live model or drama of the mythic power of the new media to alter sensibility. For this change in child behavior has nothing to do with ideas or programs.

Such a changed attitude to spatial form and presence is as definitive as the change from the photographic to the television image. In his *Prints and Visual Communication* (London: Routledge and Kegan Paul, 1953), William M. Ivins explains how the long process of capturing the external world in the "network of rationality," by the engraver's line and by ever more subtle syntax, finally reached conclusion in the photograph. The photograph is a total statement of the external object without syntax. This kind of peripety will strike the student of media as characteristic of all media development. But in television the striking fact is that the image is defined by light *through*, not by light *on*. It is this fact that separates television from photography and movie, relating it profoundly to stained glass. The spatial sense generated by television experience is utterly unlike that of the movie. And, of course, the difference has nothing to do with the "content" or the programing. Here, as ever, the medium itself is the ultimate message. The child gets such messages, when they are new, much sooner than the adult. For the adult instinctively retards awareness that will disturb a cherished order of perception or of past experience; the child would seem to have no such stake in the past, at least when he is facing new experience.

It is my point that new spatial orientation such as occurs in the format of the press after the advent of the telegraph, the swift disappearance of perspective, is also discernible in the new landscapes of Rimbaud in poetry and Cézanne in painting. And in our time Rouault anticipated the mode of the television image by decades. His use of stained glass as a means of defining the image is what I have in mind.

The mythmaking power of a medium that is itself a myth form appears now in the postliterate age as the rejection of the consumer in favor of the producer. The movie now can be seen as the peak of the consumer-oriented society, being in its form the natural means both of providing and of glorifying consumer goods and attitudes. But in the arts of the past century the swing has been away from packaging for the consumer to providing do-it-yourself kits. The spectator or reader must now be co-creator. Our educational establishment naturally lags behind the popular media in this radical change. The young, when exposed to the television image, receive at once a total orientation in spatial matters that makes the lineality of the printed word a remote and alien language. Reading for them will have to be taught as if it were heraldry or some quaint codification of reality. The assumptions about reading and writing that accompanied the monarchy of print and the related rise of industrial forms are no longer valid for, or acceptable to, those being re-formed in their sensibilities in the electronic age. To ask whether this is a good or a bad thing is to express the bias of efficient causality, which is naturally that of the man of the printed word. But it is also a futile gesture of inadequacy to the real situation. The values of the Gutenberg era cannot be salvaged by those who are as unaware of how they came into existence as they are of why they are now in the process of liquidation.

Philosophic agreement is not necessary among those who are agreed that the insistent operation of media-forms on human sensibility and awareness is an observable, intelligible, and controllable situation. Today, when ordinary consciousness is exposed to the patternmaking of several media at once, we are becoming more attentive to the unique properties of each of the media. We can see both that media are mythic "images" and that they have the power of imposing subliminally, as it were, their own assumptions. They can be viewed at the same time as intelligible explanations of great tracts of time and of the experience of many processes, and they can be used as a means of perpetuating such bias and preference as they codify in their structure.

It is not strange that we should long have been obsessed with the literary and "content" aspect of myth and media. The "form" and "content" dichotomy is as native to the abstract, written, and printed forms of codification as is the "producer" and "consumer" dichotomy.

Unfortunately for the direction and control of education, such a literary bias is quite unable to cope with the new "images" of the postliterate age. As a result of our using literary lenses, the relevant new data have escaped our scrutiny. My book, *The Mechanical Bride: Folklore of Industrial Man*, is a case in point. Turning literary guns on the new iconology of the Madison Avenue world is easy. It is easy to reveal mechanism in a postmechanical era. But I failed at that time to see that we had already passed out of the mechanistic age into the electronic, and that it was this fact that made mechanism both obtrusive and repugnant.

One of the great novelties effected by printing was the creation of a new sense of inner and outer space. We refer to it as the discovery of perspective and the rise of representation in the arts. The space of "perspective" conditioned by an artificially fixed stance for the viewer leads to the enclosing of objects in a pictorial space. Yet so revolutionary and abstract was this new space that poets avoided it in their language for two centuries after painters had accepted it. It is a kind of space very uncongenial to the media of speech and of words. One can gain some idea of the psychic pressures exerted by print in the work of William Blake, who sought new strategies of culture to reintegrate the segmented and fractured human spirit. In fact, the explicit mythmaking of Blake is the greatest monument and antidote to the mythic pressures of the printing press, to "single vision and Newton's sleep." For the matrix of movable type contains the totality of industrialism as well as the means of global conquest, which, by peripety, brought the preliterate world once more into the heart of the industrial metropolis.

The prevalent concept that the mass media exert a baneful influence on the human spirit has strange roots. As Marjorie Nicolson has shown in *Newton Demands the Muse*, it was Newton's *Opticks* that taught poets the correspondence between the inner and outer worlds, between the structure of seeing and the structure of the scene. This notion planted in poets the ambition to gain control over the inner life by a calculus of landscape composition. The idea of verbally constituted landscape, as a lever upon the psychic eye of man, was a dichotomy quite congenial to the culture of the printed word. And whereas external landscape has been abandoned for inner landscape since Rimbaud, Madison Avenue clings to the earlier Romantic concept of consumer control by means of externally arranged scenes. The recent flutter about "subliminal" advertising indicates the delayed shift of attention from outer to inner landscape that occurred in many of the arts in the later nineteenth century. And it is this same shift that today focuses attention on myth in all its modes. For myth is always a montage or transparency comprising several external spaces and times in a single image or situation. Such compression or multilayering is an inescapable mode of the electronic and simultaneous movement of information, whether in popular media or esoteric speculation. It is, therefore, an everyday occurrence for academic entertainment to stress "content," while displaying complete illiteracy with regard to media old and new. For we have now to possess many cultural languages for even the most ordinary daily purposes.

The newspaper will serve as an example of the Babel of myths or languages. When information from every quarter arrived at the same time, the paper became a daily snapshot of the globe, and "perspective" in news became meaningless. Editorials could still try to tie some items together into a chain or sequence with a special point of view or vanishing point. But such views were really capsules for passive readers, while, paradoxically, the unprocessed, uninterpreted, raw news offered far more challenge to the reader to find his own meanings. Today it is easy to see how Edgar Allen Poe, both in his symbolist poems and in his detective stories, had anticipated this new mythic dimension of producer orientation by taking the audience into the creative process itself. Likewise, it is easy to see how the spot news of the telegraph press really acts like the yes-no, black-white dots of the wirephoto in creating an inclusive world image. Yet even now the sponsors of pre-electronic media continue to overlay the new myth by injections of earlier myth, creating hybrids of the "horseless carriage" variety in the interests of superior culture.

The same type of confusion exists in education in the concept of "audio-visual aids." It would seem that we must do in education what the poets, painters, and composers have done, namely, to purge our media and test and define their unique powers before attempting Wagnerian concerts. The Gutenberg myth was not a means of modifying the Cadmus myth, any more than the Henry Ford myth modified the horse and buggy. Obliteration occurred, as it will with the movie under the impact of television, unless we choose to restrain the operation of form on form by due study and strategy. We now stand at that point with regard to all myth and media. We can, perhaps we *must*, become the masters of cultural and historical alchemy. And to this end we can, I suggest, find means in the study of media as languages and languages as myths. For our experience with the grammar and syntax of languages can be made available for the direction and control of media old and new.

The Electronic Age—The Age of Implosion

*I*t seemed obvious to Malthus that population pressed outward upon the means of subsistence. The great Newtonian discovery had been that gravity was not only inward to the centre, but outward to the margins of the system as well. For an industrializing England the means of subsistence were increasingly at the margins of the population structure. But the awareness of margins was itself a novelty of an exploding or expanding economy. To have identified the remote and unpopulous margins of an economy with the limits of the means of subsistence was a stroke of artistic genius, if only because it accommodated a large and complex area of existence to the mechanics of the then new physics of Newton.

Today, however, it is not uncommon to speak of "the old physics of Newton and Einstein." The new quantum physics is not much concerned with visual modes of perception, and least of all with the centre-margin patterns that characterized the outward radiation of the baroque explosion and colonial expansion. Today physics confronts the phenomenon of fusion and implosion rather than the outward and analytic movement of explosion. To speak of the *explosion in learning* or of the *population explosion* is scarcely relevant. Electricity has wrapped the planet in a single cohesive *field* or membrane that is organic rather than mechanical in nature. The population of the world has imploded, as have the models of perception and learning. All men are now involved in one another physically and psychically as happens when they occupy a very small village. And as global villagers, all men must now accommodate their perceptions and judgments to the complex interdependence understood and manipulated by villagers. Habits and attitudes natural to centuries of expansion now yield with equal naturalness to the intense pressures of an electronically unified world.

De Chardin in *The Phenomenon of Man* may not have been the first to observe the heart of this matter, but so far as I know he was the first to state it:

> Now, to the degree that—under the effect of this pressure and thanks to their psychic permeability—the human elements infiltrated more and more into each other, their minds (mysterious coincidence) were mutually stimulated by proximity. And as though dilated upon themselves, they each extended little by little the radius of their influence upon this earth which, by the same token, shrank steadily. What in fact do we see happening in the modern paroxysm? It has been stated over and over again. Through the discovery yesterday of the railway, the motor car and the aeroplane, the physical influence of each man, formerly restricted to a few miles, now extends to hundreds of leagues or more. Better still: thanks to the prodigious biological event represented by the discovery of electromagnetic waves, each individual finds himself henceforth (actively and passively) simultaneously present, over land and sea, in every corner of the earth.[1]

To have perceived "the prodigious biological event represented by the discovery of electromagnetic waves" is the crux. The age of mechanics that was shaped first by the technology of the phonetic alphabet, and later intensified by the logical extension of that alphabet in printing from movable types, was radically modified by the organic revolution ushered in by electricity. Centuries of stress upon the means of separating the senses of man, and of exploiting the isolated modes and properties of functions and processes, were reversed by the electromagnetic discovery.

Before taking note of characteristic traditions, derived in large part from the pre-electric means of organizing perception and experience, there is a recent testimony to obsolescence of the older mechanics which brings the process into focus:

> Nevertheless, we made an exactly counter assumption in designing machine tools of a kind that run your factories and our factories everywhere in the world. The machine tools with which we are familiar, as they become more efficient, as we expect to get greater production out of them, become larger, larger, larger, more and more specialized; they require proportionately larger commitments of capital, they require proportionately larger investments; and, in order to get the incremental cost advantage out of a new machine, one would have to, say,—instead

of making a run of one hundred of the same items—make a run of one thousand, make a run of ten thousand, make a run of one million. In consequence of this, our factories have become very large, very cumbersome; it has been very difficult to optimize the use of the productive facility, and this has been the whole trend. In fact, that businessmen, that entrepreneur who would buy a machine tool today, three years hence would be at the mercy of a competitor who bought the machine tool in the third year because, in the third year, the new machine tool would not only be more efficient but would incorporate some technological advances and even though he might have paid for the machine tool which he bought three years ago, he simply does not have the courage, the emotional bank to start all over, to tear up his factory and redesign it from scratch.

The new generation of machine tools is not like this at all. It represents a completely different set of assumptions, it represents a complete reversal of practice. And to give you examples, some very simple ones, for the new generation of tools, I would instance the new machine for making automobile tail pipe or the new machine for wiring the back panels of the IBM 1400 series of computers and machines of this type. Do you recall the publicity about the machine for making automobile tail pipes, about a year ago? Let me describe it very briefly. The older types of tools with which we are familiar are those in which there are dies, jigs, fixtures, settings, and once the settings have been made, then one would make a production run of a hundred of the same, a thousand of the same, or whatever the machine has been set for. Now, the new machine for making automobile tail pipes is about as long as the bench here in front of us, just about as wide. It has behind it a little console which is smaller than the lectern here. It has in it no dies, no fixtures, no settings of any kind. It has in it simply certain general purpose things like grippers, benders, advancers, and it is programmed by a tape. On this machine, which costs less than its predecessors as of this moment, on this machine starting just with lengths of ordinary pipe, it is possible to make eighty different kinds of tail pipe in succession, as rapidly, as easily and as cheaply as it is to make eighty of the same type. Now, this is very simple, this is very primitive, this is very childlike. But the prototypes of the new generations of machines are already in existence. Their characteristic is general purpose, flexibility, the ability to be programmed with constant changes of programme, locally, at their own place and, in consequence of this, the ability to form a whole network or a whole society of such machines in a completely flexible productive array.[2]

Muller-Thym is clear that electronic tape not only ends the assembly-line as a form of production, it restores to the individual autonomy as craftsman, as designer and as consumer. The computer makes possible a world in which all the advantages of mass production are united to those of the bespoke tailor and the artist-patron relation.

In *Fifty Years' Progress in Management: 1910–1960,* Muller-Thym contributed a chapter in which he summarized the structural characteristics of organizational change in recent decades. Since the strategies in question reflect the onset of electronic pressure on a mechanically ordered system, his observations have much relevance in this essay. For what Muller-Thym notes concerning practices in general management equally concerns practices in art, education, philosophy and science.

Business had arrived by 1950 (and for all practical purposes still is) at the point where the *rationale* of the old organizational structure could not see a manager through. One has only to recall dreary and interminable discussions of "line" and "staff," or of "functional" versus "line" authority. The farther such discussions went, the more confusion was generated. The irrationality of those discussions was clear to all who realized that the work of the company was actually being done in an informal manner outside the prescript of the organization chart. Indeed, the naive assumptions about authority itself and the manner in which it should be exercised in a work structure went increasingly counter to the national purpose and to the education and inclination of a free, multi-skilled, multi-interested work force.

ATTEMPTS AT IMPROVEMENT

Well before the 1950's as well as in this decade, there were many attempts to counter the foregoing limitations and to make the system more workable. Among these we might list:

1 Decentralization, but viewed simply as the process of "breaking big ones into smaller ones."

2 An increase in understanding of people and benevolence in managerial action introduced through human relations.

3 Development of a similarly benevolent philosophy of "delegation."

4 Attempt to find a dynamic for, or to introduce dynamics into, the system.

These attempts, which brought some measure of relief, may have shown even more clearly the need to start off on a fresh tack. In summary, the state of organizational practice by 1950, and even through much of the decade just completed, is characterized by:

1 The development of pyramidal, many-layered, highly-functionalized structures, embodying such "principles" as a span of control and the like.

2 The attempt to humanize such structures or bring them under control or help people adjust to life within them.

3 The elaboration of special bodies of "how to" knowledge—for example, how to organize the marketing function, the market research function, the district sales manager's job. . . .

These describe both the achievements and the limits of the foregoing body of practice. It would be a mistake to forget the achievement. One need only reflect on those works of Ernest Dale, Louis Allen, Robert Sampson, or Lyndall Urwick, which appeared in the 1950's, to appreciate the magnitude of the achievement. If the practice of organization has begun to move in another direction without having yet demonstrated a comparable achievement, it is because the requirements of men at work and the requirements of running a business have forced the change.[3]

One of the notable discrepancies of our time is indicated in Muller-Thym's concluding remark that "the requirements of running a business have forced the change." Such immediate motives for noting new needs resulting from new situations are normally absent from the educational and intellectual spheres. There, indeed, what Kenneth Galbraith has designated as "vested interests in acquired knowledge" are so intense that the phenomenon of *culture-lag* is the norm. The business man, paradoxically, is quicker to understand the potential of new cultural achievement than the intellectual.

In this sort of context of analysis it is easy to see how natural it was for Kenneth Galbraith to urge the business community to develop competent awareness of new art forms. For the business man may have *avant garde* motives but not necessarily adequate means of perception. It is artistic *intuition* that endows us with exact models of coming situations and makes available a kind of prescience. Wyndham Lewis has said that "the artist is engaged in writing a detailed history of the future because he alone lives in the present." For the most part men's perceptions are overlaid by patterns of past experience that render them unapt to apprehend the world they actually live in. The artist alone is an expert in the contemporary use of his senses. Properly approached, his work creates what Ulysses in Shakespeare's play calls "the providence that's in a watchful state." In *Troilus and Cressida* Ulysses tells Achilles how this statesmanlike providence

Knows almost every grain of Plutus' gold
Finds bottoms in the uncomprehensive deeps,
Keeps place with thought, and almost like the gods
Does thoughts unveil in their dumb cradles.

In the electronic age when information moves simultaneously from all quarters and from any distance, it becomes normal to perceive remote general consequences in particular innovation. Cause and effect also become simultaneous to human awareness, conferring once more a mythic dimension on consciousness. For myth is a mode of perceiving and stating causes and effects at the same time. In moral terms it is *wisdom*, or the property of oral and backward cultures, as appears in the following Asiatic anecdote of which Werner Heisenberg was fond. He records it in his book *The Physicist's Conception of Nature*:

> As Tzu-Gung was travelling through the regions north of the river Han, he saw an old man working in his vegetable garden. He had dug an irrigation ditch. The man would descend into the well, fetch up a vessel of water in his arms and pour it out into the ditch. While his efforts were tremendous the results appeared to be very meager.
>
> Tzu-Gung said, "There is a way whereby you can irrigate a hundred ditches in one day, and whereby you can do much with little effort. Would you not like to hear of it?" Then the gardener stood up, looked at him and said, "And what would that be?"
>
> Tzu-Gung replied, "You take a wooden lever, weighted at the back and light in front. In this way you can bring up water so quickly that it just gushes out. This is called a draw-well."
>
> Then anger rose up in the old man's face, and he said, "I have heard my teacher say that whoever uses machines does all his work like a machine. He who does his work like a machine grows a heart like a machine, and he who carries the heart of a machine in his breast loses his simplicity. He who has lost his simplicity becomes unsure in the strivings of his soul. Uncertainty in the strivings of the soul is something which does not agree with honest sense. It is not that I do not know of such things; I am ashamed to use them."[4]

A quantum physicist, as it were, finds a connatural affinity with the *unified field* theory of human action normal to tribal man. Western man, as I have tried to show in *The Gutenberg Galaxy*, embarked on a totally different course from tribal man. He assumed, from the new modes of perception afforded by phonetic literacy, that the pursuit of segmental and specialist patterns would be sufficiently rewarding to justify the progressive liquidation of ancient knowledge and tradition. Today, at the end of the Gutenberg era, by a kind of reversal, we find new fascination with all the pre-literate cultural modes of man. Many are now disposed to reject the entire achievement of literate Western man in an effort to recover integral values. But surely this temper is not very different from that which emerged in the early phases of literacy, when leaders were prepared to dismantle and detribalize their world in favour of a visual, lineal, individualistic stress in the organization of experience. To embark now on a reverse course is the immediate suggestion and mandate of electric technology. And to pro or con this reverse course is merely to accept the mechanical fate of a new technology. Is there no third course? How can we elude the merely technical closure in our inner lives and recover autonomy? What if any is the cultural strategy of the suspended judgment, of the open-ended proposition?

Is there the possibility of new freedom in the aesthetic response to the models of perception outered from us into our technology? If we contemplate the technological forms that we set outside ourselves as art objects, rather than as the inevitable patterns of utility, can we escape the swift *closure* of our senses? Since any new outering of ourselves is innered again with consequent displacement of sense ratios, is there any means of avoiding this displacement of inner life resulting from what Adolphe Jonas calls the "auto-amputative property?"[5]

I have in mind Kenneth Galbraith's counsel to the business man who wants to stay in business, that he should *dig* the latest art:

> Industry, alienated from the artist and with its eyes fixed by way of the market researchers on the popular taste, has regularly failed to perceive those advances in taste which were rendering its designs banal and otiose. Instead of being a little ahead, it has been a little behind.[6]

Muller-Thym, in the chapter cited earlier, shows similar awareness of the role of art in the emancipation of industrial decisions from the merely segmented and specialized packets of knowledge represented by *market research*. Thus in the case of the making of the Polaris missile he observes:

> Finally, Polaris set up two independent groups, neither on the Polaris payroll. One audited the state of art on a regular basis; it simply sifted current science and technology to see whether everything pertinent to the project was being used.[7]

Had General Motors had the equivalent wit of the Polaris makers, it could have saved North America from the chaos of outmoded and misconceived car designs that now blanket the country. Utter unawareness of the new spatial biases of the population (especially those deriving from TV) has returned the industry to the horseless carriage phase when cars were built with buggy-whip holders.

Muller-Thym's preeminence in the world of management design, like that of Peter Drucker's, is inseparable from high competence in the arts of painting, poetry and music of the past century. Both he and Drucker were once professors of philosophy. Having free access to the numerous models of perception in the arts, they transfer to the technological world all the certitude of tested artistic intuition. Knowledge of the steady increase in involvement on the part of the spectator in the process of artistic creation, since Cézanne, enables Muller-Thym to spot and validate a similar shift in management design:

> The first thing to be discovered was that pyramidal organizational structures, with many layers of supervision, and with functional division by specialty, simply did not work. The communication chain between top scientific or engineering leadership and work centres was too long for either the scientific or managerial message to be communicated. But in these research organizations where work actually got done, when one studied them he found that whatever the organization chart prescribed, groups of researchers with different competences as required by the problem in hand were working together, cutting across organizational lines; that they were establishing most of their own design criteria for the work as well as their intended patterns of association; that individually or from a working centre they arranged to tap directly into more senior sources of competence; and that the patterns of their group association at work followed the organization of their competences as human knowledges.[8]

Another way of stating the change is to say that when information movement speeds up a great deal, centre-margin patterns yield to centres-without-margins. A centre-margin structure, whether in empires or in private perception, is one in which there is very little interplay at the margins. The margins become areas of specialism and relative fixity of form, as in colonies. Innovation and interplay are at the centre. Such tends to be the norm of structure in the pre-electric period of mechanical and industrial organization.

The unavoidable dynamic of centre-margin structure when an efficient centralism of roads and couriers is developed, is just as natural as decentralized centres-without-margins when such roads and couriers are discouraged. That is to say, the clash between Rome and Byzantium features the very same difference that now grows apace within the heart of modern organizations at every level. The

words of Steven Runciman in *The Sicilian Vespers* will illuminate the
issue:

> The true danger to the Popes was not what they had feared. It was not
> that the Empire might triumph, but that in destroying the Empire the
> Papacy itself might commit suicide.
>
> A wise spectator might have seen that the day of the old international
> Empire was over. The longing of mankind for the tranquillity and peace
> that one universal state should produce had not faded; nor will it ever
> fade. But the difficulties of achieving unity were now more obvious.
> Racial needs and traditions were pulling centrifugally; poor
> communications had created too many barriers. New and smaller units
> were forming, based on the practical demands of geography. The
> Emperor, despite his oecumenical title, was merely the king of the lands
> of middle Europe, and a king whose authority was dependent on a
> superimposed idea, unlike his brothers of France or England, whose
> power was firmly rooted in reality. The Empire was to find its most
> eloquent advocates during the next century; but they preached a lost
> cause. The future lay with national kingdoms.[9]

Decentralism today is the child of space-time and instantaneous
information movement. In the Middle Ages it was the child of the
opposite factor—retarded communications and the disappearance of
paper that made the centre-margin structure of the Roman empire
baseless and inoperative.

Under conditions of simultaneous access to information, regardless of distances, or since telegraph and telephone, those kinds of
organization devised for slower information movement certainly
prove unworkable. A striking instance of the kind of structural innovation resulting from telegraph and telephone is stated by Peter
Drucker in *Landmarks of Tomorrow*:

> We still express the structure of authority, responsibility, function and
> rank in organization in the typical organization chart, which shows the
> chief executive at the top and the lesser executives as exercising
> authority delegated by him. It is still customary to explain the existence
> of organization by the fact that there is more work to be done than any
> man can do, so that he has to delegate to others what is really part of
> his job.
>
> But this is nonsense in modern organization. The individual people
> of skill, knowledge and judgment cannot exercise somebody else's
> authority or somebody else's knowledge. They exercise their own
> knowledge and should have the authority that befits their contribution. It
> is the job that determines the authority and responsibility of the holder—

and this is original authority grounded in the needs and objective
requirements for performance rather than in the power of the man
above.[10]

No theoretic change is involved. The older pattern won't work under
electric conditions so it is altered. And to alter the structure of
authority from delegation and specialism to a pattern based on "the
authority of knowledge" requires that all personnel have very much
more knowledge of the entire structure and operation. Hence industry now cries out for crowds of new PH.D.'s in anything at all, that is
for people able to accept high level training.

The old structure of delegated authority and specialized jobs did
not demand people of inclusive consciousness and powers of ready
inter-relation. The new executive has to be a person with an ever
wider range of awareness, and he looks to the educational establishment to widen and deepen its entire operation to this end. But the
educational establishment has built up its centre-margin patterns
very slowly and has a huge stake in its specialized forms of acquired
knowledge. Moreover, it does not acknowledge the urgency of the
pressures that are felt by the business community. Drucker states the
matter clearly:

> Any man of professional standing in the modern organization, whether
> he be manager or individual professional, has three equally important
> responsibilities. Each of them then needs its own authority. He has a
> responsibility to make it possible for subordinates to do their own work
> most effectively. He has a responsibility to the entire organization. And
> he has a responsibility to people who do not stand in any authority
> relationship to him, who work in other areas and in other jobs, and who
> yet depend on him for knowledge, information, advice, ideas or
> teaching.
>
> Here is a subtle structure. Rank, authority, function and rewards are all
> distinct rather than inseparable as they have always been. This structure
> answers no known organization design. It has a pattern of its own. Its
> emergence is both a result of the new world-view of pattern and
> process and in itself a major part of it.
>
> In asking for the principle of the new organization we ask for the
> principle of human order in society. The elements of this new
> configuration, which we have here called the "new organization," are
> human beings. Its process is human dedication, human knowledge and
> human effort. Its purpose is the creation and satisfaction of human
> values. And its principle of organization must therefore be a vision of
> man in society.[11]

The educational establishment characteristically feels the new pressures at the student level. Increasing loss of student attention and motivation in the classroom corresponds to the loss of efficiency and income in a business. But the teacher is less inclined than the business man to seek the real causes. Teachers are likely to assign moral causes for the decline of student interest. Just how irrelevant such *moral* factors may be appears in another connection altogether. The economist Robert Theobald in *The Challenge of Abundance* confronts the clash of structures as between rich and poor countries. Today *economic aid* for poor countries is fraught with paradoxical disaster because the patterns of action and motivation in the two kinds of economies are opposed. Backward countries have never developed the consumer incentives natural to our specialist economy. Our industrial complex was built on the pyramid of segmented tasks and authorities possible in highly literate societies. Yet, under electronic conditions of implosion or close inter-relation, we now begin to experience on a global scale the very same clash of patterns that Drucker and Muller-Thym have described as already existing at the very core of our own managerial complex. The *backward* countries are still in that stage of pre-specialism and overall awareness that has become mandatory in the electric phase of our new electrically speeded industry. Economic analysts looking at these countries are struck as much by the contemporary relevance of their traditional patterns as by their lack of mechanical *know-how*. Theobald puts it this way:

> The problem facing us is to decide how much emphasis the poor countries should lay on the need for economic growth, how drastically they should revise their social system to encourage economic growth. The most vital difference between the rich and poor countries is that the poor countries have not attached much importance to economic growth in the past and are not organized to encourage the changes required if they are to attain it. Economic growth in the Western countries, in Russia, and in Japan resulted from the dissolution and destruction of social patterns that limited the rate of change in response to economic forces. In America, where this process has gone furthest, the individual often moves his home every two or three years, leaving behind him all but his immediate family. This caused a major—if little noticed—revolution that separates the generation born around the turn of the century from those born between the two World Wars. The older generation typically knew every limb of its family tree, and can trace all the great-uncles and

second cousins twice-removed. To the younger generation this is slightly amusing or downright ridiculous: the family usually consists of husband, wife, and children. Some residual loyalty may remain for one's parents and perhaps for brothers and sisters, but this is the normal limit of interest.

Many people will go where their jobs take them—their work is the controlling factor in their lives. If one line of industry declines, people are increasingly willing to enter another—they feel no emotional bond with their trade or even their profession. The concept of man as a unit of labour is still gaining ground simply because men have subordinated their social interests to their economic—we have made arrangements that allow men to be used "efficiently" and moved from one occupation to another with the minimum of difficulty.[12]

A century ago an economic observer would have had no qualms about prescribing the full mechanical *explosion* programme for *backward* areas. Today in an imploded world our new sense of the interdependence of needs, skills and satisfactions in the shaping of human order inclines us to caution and conservatism in approaching traditional societies. It would be a mistake to ascribe this difference to a change of heart or of values on our part. Rather it is our perceptions that have altered. Under conditions of the electric speed of knowledge we cannot choose but note patterns of inclusive order. Such patterns were not perceptible a century ago, save to poets and artists.

The horror felt by William Blake, who lived at the centre of the industrial explosion, is now regarded as prophetic. But any kind of awareness is prophetic among populations percussed by new media explosions, for all new outerings of our senses and faculties that are new technologies and new media arrive in a series of explosions. Whether it is the wheel, the alphabet or radio, each brings into existence at once a series of new enterprises. But the thing itself creates numbness at the point of impact. That all of our technologies are ablations of our faculties, Edward T. Hall explains in *The Silent Language*:

Today man has developed extensions for practically everything he used to do with his body. The evolution of weapons begins with the teeth and the fist and ends with the atom bomb. Clothing and houses are extensions of man's biological temperature-control mechanisms. Furniture takes the place of squatting and sitting on the ground. Power tools, glasses, TV, telephones, and books which carry the voice across both time and space are examples of material extensions. Money is a

way of extending and storing labour. Our transportation networks now
do what we used to do with our feet and backs. In fact, all man-made
material things can be treated as extensions of what man once did with
his body or some specialized part of his body.[13]

But the ablated or outered faculty returns to plague the inventor.
The outered sense or faculty must be *innered* by the human community in the ordinary course of perception. And when it enters the
human system again there is large displacement of the other senses
and faculties, as William Blake spent his life proclaiming in vain.
Mark Schorer explains this in *William Blake: The Politics of Vision*,
when he discusses how the act of perception itself is the main subject
of most of his poems. It is especially significant that Blake saw this act
as metamorphic and transforming, for it is this metamorphic factor
in perception that was unacceptable to Blake's well-wishers then and
since:

It is the first feature in his picture of himself, and "perception," as a result,
is the real subject of most of his poems. Blake's longest work, *Jerusalem*,
is a poem about perception and reality; its most frequently repeated line
is "They became what they beheld." At the very peak of the narrative he
exclaims:
> . . . & every Word & every Character
> Was Human according to the Expansion or Contraction, the
> Translucence or
> Opakeness of Nervous fibres: such was the variation of
> Time & Space
> Which vary according as the Organs of Perception vary.

"Perception," likewise, is the subject of much of the poetry of Blake's
contemporaries. Coleridge's lines in "Dejection"—
> O Wordsworth! we receive but what we give,
> And in our life alone does Nature live—

have more than a merely fortuitous value to the understanding of Blake's
vision.[14]

Having outered ourselves in new materials we have to behold ourselves anew. And we then become what we behold. This was Blake's
mythic version of social change. The innering of ourselves (cf. the
Trojans and the Wooden Horse) necessarily shatters any existing
equilibrium or ratio among our senses and faculties, destroying the
interplay that is the life of the eternal imagination by giving great
stress to one sense or faculty alone. This had happened with the
visual sense in the Renaissance, leading to "single vision and

Newton's sleep." The technologically percussed society is hynotically entranced, and quite unable to perceive its own condition.

In the electronic age with the outering of all five senses, we turn to the outering of mental operations in computers. But with the externalization of the haptic or tactile faculty in the TV image[15] it is possible that a kind of ratio among the five outered senses could be established. But this would require a full awareness of our condition that has resulted from the outering of all our senses, and such awareness we isolate in the artist alone, seeing to it that he remains helpless to guide the perceptions or judgment of his society.

Today the hypnotized and somnambulistic citizen, percussed by the electronic implosion in general and the TV image in particular, typically responds with the moral panic of the Vance Packards and Daniel Boorstins. A fixed position from which to gaze at the current *plasma* of superheated events is consistent with the old technology of "single vision and Newton's sleep." A fixed point of view yields what E. H. Gombrich calls "the anguish of the third dimension." It is based on the isolation of the visual sense from the interplay of the other senses, and it never seeks nor finds insight into the actual structure of any situation. By substituting point of view for insight we trap ourselves in a single isolated sense, as is shown at length in *The Gutenberg Galaxy*. This point of view is always accompanied by a sound track of hebdomadal moralizing.

Daniel Boorstin in *The Image* has a rich field for this purpose since he has only to compare the present electric age with the previous mechanical age in order to have a ready-made series of events that register a lamentable decline of values. On every front, in every department of daily life, acceleration of information and services has translated us from a simple straightforward pattern of effort and rewards into a crazy mosaic of contradictions: "We expect compact cars which are spacious; luxurious cars which are economical."[16] Morally, we expect to be "powerful and merciful, active and reflective."[17] And having long lived in a mechanistic culture of one-thing-at-a-time, such contradictions strike Professor Boorstin as a mark of irrationalism. But to an electric age the contradictory polarities of a "total field" are necessary to the structure, so that we really do plan to eat and stay thin, to be kind and competitive. Especially do we expect to be specialist and universalist, to be deeply involved or participant, yet autonomous.

Professor Boorstin is quite right in detecting in the new simultaneous world of the *Image* something different from "the American
Dream." That fact comes out very strongly in Douglas Cater's *The
Fourth Branch of Government*, from which Boorstin admittedly derives
much of his approach to the "pseudo-event" as characteristic of our
new world. Douglas Cater as a news reporter in Washington
describes the ever-changing techniques by which a deliberately fragmented plan of government ("separation of powers") adapts itself to
the seamless web of an electronic world. The translation of fragmented government powers and procedures into the unified mosaic
of the daily press is a miracle of virtuoso pigmentation. Literally, this
pigment is extracted from the fragmented and rivalry-ridden government departments by the pressures of "the news-leak." Since the
press exists to publicize what most government departments need
desperately to keep private and to themselves, the technique of the
news-leak as non-committal testing of various attitudes and pressures
is indispensable. The press as sheer agent of publicity is part of the
older Gutenberg technology of dynamic mechanism by fragmentation. On the other hand, secrecy as the dominant force in any pattern
of coalition and diplomatic interplay is a central feature of the electric age, as any stockbroker knows as well as does any diplomat.

Secrecy, precise timing of information, is inevitable in the electric age, just because everything has instant effect on everything else.
How then can a mechanistic world of publicity and fragmented government departments co-exist with an electric world of secrecy
except by the news-leak? For the "leak" is only an artistic daub at a
canvas or mosaic. The *effect* on the total picture and on the audience
is what has to be discovered by the leak. Reporter, politician, and PR
man alike have now to use the media experimentally for testing of
audience effects. And as the artist cannot know what he wants to say
until he has said it, the reporter and the politician are now in the
same situation. Their private point of view becomes merely one
shade of pigment.

To both Daniel Boorstin and Douglas Cater, the incongruities
resulting from the clash of mechanical and electric cultures enable
them to shower us with the paradoxical images of decline in our daily
lives. Thus in the mechanical age a man was famous for having done
something. Today he is famous for being well known. In an age of

information movement, fame is literally being known for being well known. The Graphic Revolution, by which a private image can be showered on the world overnight, scrambles and confuses all pre-electric categories of fame and greatness. But it also increases the demand for big names and big images. Let us keep in mind that the new reality is in the image and not behind it. This simple fact the literary and book-oriented man finds hard to accept. In the world of the book it is always the man back of the book who *seems* to be the important fact. This is an illusion of the book medium that is only too often discovered. For authors put the best of themselves into their books, if only out of vanity, and save very little for private life. But a literary culture not only refuses to learn the language of the graphic media; it delights in bemoaning the lack of "depth" in these graphic gods, as a vocalist might deplore the lack of resonance in the printed page.

Individual fame and notoriety in the modern sense began with Aretino and the printing press. The mechanical technology was necessary to create and extend the authorial image. Authors, under manuscript conditions, were very vague composite entities. But it is true that with photography and electronics it became possible to bypass the consumer phase in fame. One could simply become famous or celebrated for being famous or celebrated, without going through the tedious process of discovering and peddling some marketable commodity or entertaining stereotype. It was now possible to shift the commodity *fame* from the consumer to the producer phase. Anybody or anything can now be *made* famous. Professor Boorstin disapproves of this distinction: "Some analysts say the shift is primarily the sign of a new focus of popular attention away from production and toward consumption. But this is oversubtle."[18]

If the difference between producer and consumer orientation is *oversubtle* it is easy to see why Professor Boorstin prefers to remain in the old mechanical culture with its uncommunicating and fragmented apertures or points of view. Seen through the fragmented apertures, both old and new worlds assume the character of what Professor Boorstin calls *pseudo-events.* Seen in inter-relation, however, all culture is a pseudo-event. Languages are vast accumulations of pseudo-events or fictions that in turn distort all the experience of those using languages. But all Professor Boorstin means by a *pseudo-event* is the pattern of implosion, or contraction of time, space and knowledge by electronic speeds of information movement.

By contrast to these *pseudo-events* Professor Boorstin is prepared to consider as real events those that get reported more slowly. But more than a century ago newspaper editors discovered that *news* is what gets printed. If it isn't in print it isn't news. Erik Barnouw in *Mass Communication* explained the history of this discovery:

> It is not surprising that the journalisitic tradition of lashing "the rascals naked through the world" continued with rising intensity through these years of turmoil. For everyone's troubles, the papers provided satisfying scapegoats: trusts, politicians, unions, anarchists, saloonkeepers, foreigners.
>
> The *Journal*, under William Randolph Hearst, was not content with exposure. The *Journal* adopted the slogan: "While others talk, the *Journal* acts." The *Journal* claimed credit for solving a murder. It brought suit in the courts to correct evil conditions. In 1898, when the battleship *Maine* exploded in the harbour of Havana, it offered fifty thousand dollars reward for information. Headlines screamed: "THE WARSHIP *MAINE* WAS SPLIT IN TWO BY AN ENEMY'S SECRET INFERNAL MACHINE." It developed feeling to such a fever pitch that when war began, the *Journal* was felt to have forced the nation's hand and made war inevitable. The *Journal's* circulation passed one million.
>
> A hundred years earlier, at the beginning of the nineteenth century, papers had waited for news to come to them. By mid-century they were sending reporters everywhere in search of news. By the end of the century they were making news.
>
> Making news now began to grow into a major occupation. But a new figure was to take over.
>
> The growing power of the press was giving impetus to a novel type of middleman. The *press agent* had for some time existed in the circus field, but not in business.[19]

Professor Boorstin has not adapted his perceptions to electronic conditions, so that he experiences the world as a Marx Brothers show by looking at the new electric technology through the old mechanical lenses.

But Boorstin's case is typical of the educational community as well. For example, in his *Process of Education* Professor Jerome Bruner insists that teaching must now shift from the present narrative mode to a structural one. But Bruner seems quite unaware that the teaching procedures of recent decades had any structure of their own. As much as Boorstin, he is unconscious of his own cultural assumptions.

And by *structural* Professor Bruner means *depth* or multi-levelled, rather than the approach by description and narrative. In fact Bruner prescribes the same approach in 1960 that Cézanne and Baudelaire had adopted in 1860. That is to say, it is a haptic or tactile and synesthetic approach, rather than a visual one. When the painter presents his world as if the viewer held it in his hands, rather than as if he merely saw it, that is the *depth* approach, or structuralism. It involves the viewer or learner much more in an act of participation than does the merely visual approach. Thus, an abstract painting is one that offers little to the viewer as consumer, but does suggest how the viewer can be co-creator, and become involved in the creative process itself. Edgar Allan Poe made the same discovery in the symbolist poem and the detective story; in both the reader is necessarily co-creator.

It is precisely the role of co-creator that we saw causing consternation in the mind of Professor Boorstin. Anything more or less than a completed consumer package strikes him as a *pseudo-event*. Bruner on the other hand greets the co-creator role, the haptic or structural approach, with a cheer. Does he imagine that the pre-structural pattern that constitutes our culture, education and politics will remain much as it is when we introduce the structural or depth approach to existing subjects? The business community has no such illusion when it makes the same shift from fragmented or delegated authority to depth and the "authority of knowledge." But the business community has long been accustomed to planned obsolescence and to the scrapping of expensive plant and installations. It would be more reassuring if innovators like Professor Bruner showed awareness of the cultural assumptions in the structures they were prepared to scrap. Likewise, if Bruner were familiar with the new mythic dimensions of the art and technology of the past century he would be better able to appraise the degree of brain-washing involved in his structural programme. It is entirely true that any subject whatsoever when pursued in depth ceases to be a *subject* and takes unto itself the totality of knowledge. Even on a modest scale the depth or structural approach represents the now familiar mode of electronic implosion. For five centuries life and learning have moved on the opposite assumption of explosion, or of separation of sense and faculty and subjects. Implosion reverses all those fragmented patterns of sequential and homogenized data. Implosion means the end of the teacher as expounder and of the lecture as briefing session. Instead of the teacher of a subject, the pattern shifts under implosion to the small team devoted (Operations Research style) to a live problem. The dialogue supplants the exposition, and even the elementary student turns from the consumption of existing knowledge to top-level research.

Robert Oppenheimer is reported to have said: "There are children here in the street whose perception could penetrate some of my most baffling problems in physics." And this is a simple fact attested to by the performance of Operations Research teams. For in many of these teams highly trained individuals are systematically excluded as unable to face new situations with candid gaze.

John Dewey's idea of a fusion of school and society tended to be merely a consumer operation, much like the *audio-visual aids* approach to the present curriculum. It was an idea of enrichment and augmentation within the existing structure. But the electronic implosion when it reaches the school and the curriculum will have the same effect there that it has already had in reversing the structure of management and decision-making in the business world. There will be no more classrooms and no schools and no subjects. School and classroom as we know them were the direct extension of the technology of the printed book. And the printed book was the first teaching-machine, whereas the manuscript had been merely a teaching tool. The printed book as a uniformly repeatable commodity made possible a new kind of learning process. It became *natural* to have the same book in every student's hands, and the educational goal gradually became the homogenization of national populations. By the same token the printed book made possible much sub-division and partitioning of *subjects* that had previously been included in major *disciplines*. *Grammatica* included all that we now associate with cultural history and the *new criticism*. *Dialectica* embraced the whole range of scientific theory and classification. *Rhetorica* involved the arts of wisdom and eloquence extended to all fields. The experience of implosion today is already characterized by new respect for the old trivium, and by an even more synthetic *field* approach to language and communication in general than was achieved in the ancient trivium. In fact structural linguistics today by means of the tape-recorder extends grammar and language study to every facet and assumption of perception and sensibility in an entire cultural system. Moreover, it renders access to the entire system very speedy and precise.

In the same way as the entire globe becomes a single computer or what de Chardin calls a *noosphere*, the advent of satellite broadcasting makes every one of the more than two hundred and fifty cultures of the globe as immediately present to each other as are the telephone subscribers of a single town. The dialogue between cultures will become as pervasive as back-fence gossiping. But, as information movement expands in this plenary way, the business and politics and diversions of mankind fuse into a single uninterrupted action. Wealth that had previously depended on the *changes* wrought by nature in the growth of plants and animals, and later by the *exchange* of these changes, now becomes the by-product of the exchange of information itself. Wealth is already derived for the most part from the movement of information alone, and will increase in our time as the mere reflex of human chatter. That is why paid learning is long overdue. Whereas in previous ages higher education was a luxury or a privilege, it has become today a necessity of ordinary production and perception, and since knowledge has become the source of wealth and power, all those engaged in learning anything at all, from kindergarten onwards, are eligible for full adult payment. Indeed, without such paid learning our new economy is quite unable to release its riches for communal use. But we persist in thinking of education as a cost or charge upon the community, exactly as it has been defined in the preceding mechanical age. As our technology begins to tackle the light barrier, our concepts hobble toward the challenge of the archaic oat-barrier, as it were.

Many economists such as Gerard Piel have noted our unpreparedness of mind as we move deeper into a workless and propertyless society. It is almost as disconcerting as trying to image an economy without weaponry. In an essay entitled "Consumers of Abundance," Gerard Piel writes:

> The advance of science has for many years been undermining the two pillars of our economy—property and work. Each at length has fallen from its place. Property is no longer the primary source of economic

power, and ownership no longer establishes the significant, functioning connection between people and the things they consume. Work occupies fewer hours and years in the lives of everyone; what work there is grows less like work every year, and the less the people work, the more their product grows. In the place of work and property, illusions and old habits and compulsions now support the social edifice. Public understanding must eventually overtake this transformation in the relationship of modern man to his physical environment. Fundamental changes in the social order—in man's relationship to man—are therefore in prospect and are already in process.[20]

In terms of present organization and concepts a warless society would be as disconcerting as a propertyless one. In a section of *A World Without War*, Walter Millis noted:

War and fear have operated powerfully in the promotion of technology and to a lesser extent in the promotion of science and education. The unlocking of nuclear energy, while by far the greatest, is by no means the only major scientific-technical achievement attributable directly to the pressures of war. With the powerful stimuli of war and the war system removed, would progress in knowledge, in science and in technology tend to slow down? There are no doubt many who would be inclined to welcome a slackening in the pace of scientific and technological advance, already moving so rapidly as to create more problems than it solves; but whether that result is to be desired or feared, it is doubtful that the abolition of war would have much effect in the matter. The elimination of war could not eliminate competition of various kinds between the great power centres; and if we no longer needed weapons systems, our need for the weapons of the mind would be only the more intense.[21]

And William O. Douglas comments in the same volume:

The dependency of nations on each other is developing international collectivism in myriad forms. This is a healthy growth of collectivism of which the free world is a part. It is, indeed, one of the aims of the United Nations as expressed in Article I, "to achieve international co-operations in solving international problems of an economic, social, cultural or humanitarian character." The development of supranational institutions of an administrative character will in time result in the emergence of patterns or codes of administrative procedure.[22]

The authors of this book are quite aware that the problem of war and peace today is a cetripetal and not a centrifugal problem. And the centripetal dynamic is pluralistic, not uniform nor centralist. Yet the entire experience of literate man disposes him toward uniform centralist and homogeneous patterns of organization. Literate man, in short, is ill-equipped to perceive the character of the problems facing electronic man.

> No one seriously believes today that it is possible to "protect investments" by landing Marines, nor does anyone in the smaller nations believe that organized war upon the imperial power is the only, or even the best, way to recover control of the nation's capital supply. The abortive Anglo-French descent upon Suez is very probably the last adventure of the kind that we shall see.[23]

In the mechanical age of centre-margin structure, Fidel Castro could not have occurred. In the electronic age of centres-without margins he can be a power. The new structure is not the old sponge pattern of intake from the margins and output from the centre, but of dialogue among centres. This is the shape of the Common Market, a post-mechanical type of organization such as also flourished in the Byzantine world before the Renaissance.

It was said by A. N. Whitehead, in *Science and the Modern World*, that "the greatest invention of the nineteenth century was the invention of the method of invention." He develops the observation as follows:

> A new method entered into life. In order to understand our epoch, we can neglect all the details of change, such as railways, telegraphs, radios, spinning machines, synthetic dyes. We must concentrate on the method in itself; that is the real novelty, which has broken up the foundations of the old civilization. The prophecy of Francis Bacon has now been fulfilled; and man, who at times dreamt of himself as a little lower than the angels, has submitted to become the servant and the minister of nature. It still remains to be seen whether the same actor can play both parts.
>
> The whole change has arisen from the new scientific information. Science, conceived not so much in its principles as in its results, is an obvious storehouse of ideas for utilization. But, if we are to understand what happened during the century, the analogy of a mine is better than that of a storehouse. Also, it is a great mistake to think that the bare scientific idea is the required invention, so that it has only to be picked up and used. An intense period of imaginative design lies between. One element in the new method is just the discovery of how to set about bridging the gap between the scientific ideas, and the ultimate product. It is a process of disciplined attack upon one difficulty after another.[24]

Another way of saying this in terms of the art process was given by T. S. Eliot in his essay on *Hamlet*:

The only way of expressing emotion in the form of art is by finding an "objective correlative"; in other words, a set of objects, a situation, a chain of events which shall be the formula of that *particular* emotion; such that when the external facts, which must terminate in sensory experience, are given, the emotion is immediately invoked.

It has been said on the other hand that the greatest discovery of the twentieth century has been that of the technique of the suspended judgment. This means the technique for avoiding the consequences or the *closure*, as Mr. Eliot describes above. We now can foresee the consequences of any kind of situation so fully that it is no longer necessary to have the *experience* at all. We are inclined to regard such experience as merely a trap for the unwary, or for somnambulists. I would suggest that the power to foresee and to forestall in this way is inevitable in the electronic age. At the present phase of the electronic age we are merely percussed by the latest outering of our senses in the TV image—to wit our sense of touch.

ACOUSTIC SPACE

*W*e often have difficulty in understanding a purely verbal
notion. In *Alice in Wonderland*:

" '. . . the patriotic archbishop of Canterbury, found it advis-
able——' "

"Found *what*?" said the Duck.

"Found *it*," the Mouse replied rather crossly: "of course you
know what 'it' means."

"I know what 'it' means well enough, when *I* find a thing," said
the Duck: "it's generally a frog or a worm. The question is, what did
the archbishop find?"

We feel happier when *it* is visible; then it's oriented in a way we
understand. For, in our workaday world, space is conceived in terms
of that which separates visible objects. "Empty space" suggests a
field in which there is nothing *to see*. We refer to a gasoline drum
filled with pungent fumes or to a tundra swept by howling gales as
"empty" because nothing is visible in either case.

Not all cultures think this way. In many preliterate cultures the
binding power of oral tradition is so strong that the eye is sub-
servient to the ear. In the beginning was the Word: a spoken word,
not the visual one of literate man. Among the Eskimo, there is no
silent sculpture. Idols are unknown; instead, deities are masked
dancers who *speak* and *sing*. When the mask speaks it contains meaning and value; silent, static—illustrated in a book or hung in a
museum—it is empty of value.

In our society, however, to be real, a thing must be visible, and
preferably constant. We trust the eye, not the ear. Not since
Aristotle assured his *readers* that the sense of sight was "above all others" the one to be trusted, have we accorded to sound a primary role.

"Seeing is believing." "Believe half of what you see and nothing of what you hear." "The eyes of the Lord preserve knowledge, and he over-throweth the words of the transgressor." [Proverbs 22:12]. Truth, we think, must be observed by the "eye," then judged by the "I." Mysticism, intuition, are bad words among scientists. Most of our thinking is done in terms of *visual* models, even when an auditory one might prove more efficient. We employ spatial metaphor even for such psychological states as tendency, duration, intensity. We say "thereafter," not the more logical "thenafter"; "always" means "at all times"; "before" means etymologically "in front of"; we even speak of a "space" or an "interval" of time.

To the Eskimo, truth is given through oral tradition, mysticism, intuition, all cognition, not simply by observation and measurement of physical phenomena. To them, the ocularly visible apparition is not nearly as common as the purely auditory one; *hearer* would be a better term than *seer* for their holy men.

Now, every normal person, regardless of culture, spends the greater part of his waking activity in a visual world of three dimensions. If he thinks about the matter at all, he is inclined to conclude that this is the way, the only way, the world is made. It is therefore worth recalling that the child must *learn* to see the world as we know it. At or shortly after birth, his eyes are as perfectly developed a camera mechanism as they will ever be. In a sense they are too perfect and too mechanical, since they present him with a world in which everything is inverted, double, laterally reversed, and devoid of depth. In the course of time, by a tremendous tour de force of learning, he turns the world right side up, achieves binocular fusion, and reverses the lateral field so that he now sees his father as one person, erect, whole, and bilaterally oriented.

At the same time his growing capacity for movement leads him to explore this visual panorama tactually and kinesthetically. This activity is the basis of the development of the dominant characteristic of visual experience: depth. Without motor movement and its attendant kinesthesis, it is hard, if not impossible, to believe that depth perception would develop at all. Imagine a child incapable of motion from birth: that child would live in the two-dimensional world of its own retinae. No identifiable person or object, as such, could emerge for him, since, as his mother approached, she would appear as several different people of progressively greater size. Nor could such a child develop an awareness of himself. Even the congenitally blind child is not so handicapped: he has auditory space in which to function unimpaired by the hopeless visual conflicts of the hypothetical child, and, more importantly, he can explore this auditory world tactually while in motion. In other words, the chief characteristic of visual space—depth—is not primarily derived from visual experience at all, but comes rather from locomotion and its attendant kinesthesis.

We suppress or ignore much of the world as visually given in order to locate and identify *objects* in three dimensions. It is the objects which compel our attention and orient our behavior; space becomes merely that which must be traversed in getting to or from them. It exists between them, but they define it. Without them you have empty space. Most people feel an obscure gratitude to Einstein because he is said to have demonstrated that "infinite" space has a boundary of some kind. The gratitude flows, not because anyone understands how this can be, but because it restores to visual space one of its essential elements.

The essential feature of sound, however, is not its location, but that it *be*, that it fill space. We say "the night shall be filled with music," just as the air is filled with fragrance; locality is irrelevant. The concert-goer closes his eyes.

Auditory space has no point of favored focus. It's a sphere without fixed boundaries, space made by the thing itself, not space containing the thing. It is not pictorial space, boxed in, but dynamic, always in flux, creating its own dimensions moment by moment. It has no fixed boundaries; it is indifferent to background. The eye focuses, pinpoints, abstracts, locating each object in physical space, against a background; the ear, however, favors sound from any direction. We hear equally well from right or left, front or back, above or below. If we lie down, it makes no difference, whereas in visual space the entire spectacle is altered. We can shut out the visual field by simply closing our eyes, but we are always triggered to respond to sound.

Audition has boundaries only in terms of upper and lower thresholds. We hear waves produced by double vibration cycles of about 16 cycles per second up to about 20,000 per second. The amount of energy needed to produce an auditory sensation is so small

that, were the ears just slightly more sensitive, we could hear mole-
cules of air crashing into each other, provided, of course, we could
learn to ignore the continuous Niagara of sound such ears would
detect in the circulation of blood!

Auditory space has no boundaries in the visual sense. The distance a sound can be heard is dictated more by its intensity than by
the capacity of the ear. We might compare this to looking at a star,
where visual sensation, transcending the vanishing point, is achieved,
but at the sacrifice of the precise framework we call visual space.
There is nothing in auditory space corresponding to the vanishing
point in visual perspective. One can, with practice, learn to locate
many objects by sound, but this can be done so much better by vision
that few of us bother. We continue to be amazed at the "psychic"
powers of the blind, who establish direction and orientation by translating auditory-tactual clues into the visual knowledge they once had,
an orientation infinitely more difficult for the congenitally blind.

In general, auditory space lacks the precision of visual orientation. It is easy, of course, to determine whether a sound comes from
the right or left, because the width of the head makes it inevitable
that the ears be stimulated by slightly different phases of the wave (a
difference of 16/10,000 of a second can be detected). But it is impossible, while blindfolded, to judge accurately whether a neutral
buzzer, at a constant distance, is directly before or behind one and,
similarly, whether directly overhead or underfoot.

The universe is the potential map of auditory space. We are not
Argus-eyed, but we are Argus-eared. We hear instantly anything
from any direction and at any distance, within very wide limits. Our
first response to such sensation is to move head and body to train our
eyes on the source of the sound. Thus the two sense avenues coordi-
nate as a team, each supplying an essential element for survival that
the other lacks. Whereas the eyes are bounded, directed, and limited
to considerably less than half the visible world at any given moment,
the ears are all encompassing, constantly alert to any sound originating in their boundless sphere.

The ear is closely affiliated with man's emotional life, originally
in terms of survival. The "sudden loud sound" that Watson thought
produced an instinctive (unlearned) fear response in the infant still
compels our quick (conditioned) fear response when perceived as,

say, an automobile horn. It's the ambulance siren, not the blinker, that first warns us. Of what use would it be for a taxi driver to wave a flag or resort to any other visual equivalent for a warning? The onrushing cab itself is sufficient warning—if you happen to be looking that way! The dimensionless space of auditory sensation is the only hope in this circumstance; precisely because it is directionless, any sudden sound, from any quarter, will be attended to instantly.

Not all sounds are sudden, and not all are fear-producing. Auditory space has the capacity to elicit the gamut of emotions from us, from the marching song to opera. It can be filled with sound that has no "object," such as the eye demands. It need not be representational, but can speak, as it were, directly to emotion. Music can, of course, be visually evocative, as program music is, or it can be made to subserve the ends of visual presentation, as in the case of tin-pan alley tunes invented or stolen to fit lyrics. But there is no demand that music do either.

Poets have long used the word as incantation, evoking the visual image by magical acoustic stress. Preliterate man was conscious of this power of the auditory to make present the absent thing. Writing annulled this magic because it was a rival magical means of making present the absent sound. Radio restored it. In fact, in evoking the visual image, radio is sometimes more effective than sight itself. The squeaking door in *Inner Sanctum* was far more terrifying over radio than that same door seen and heard on television, because the visual image that sound evokes comes from the imagination.

This interplay between sense perceptions creates a redundancy, where, even if one element of a pattern is omitted, it is nevertheless implied. We feel, hear, and see "flaming, crackling red." Leave out "red," and it's still there; green neither flames nor crackles. In *The Eve of St. Agnes*, Keats describes how objects feel, taste, sound, and smell:

> . . . her vespers done,
> Of all its wreathed pearls her hair she frees;
> Unclasps her warmed jewels one by one;
> Loosens her fragrant boddice; by degrees
> Her rich attire creeps rustling to her knees. . . .

Elsewhere he describes fruit in terms of smell, taste, touch, even sound, and thus we experience the fruit; he uses lots of *l*'s and *o*'s and *u*'s; the mouth drips with honey as it forms these sounds.

This sort of interplay creates a dynamic process—being alive, the ritual drama—particularly in primitive societies where the association of elements in such patterns is especially strong. Much of the intellectual excitement of 5th century Athens related to the discovery of the visual world and the translation of oral tradition into written and visual modes (probably the new role of the eye was as exciting to the Greeks as television is to us). The medieval world tried to channel the acoustic via Gregorian and liturgical chants, but it expanded into the visual world, and the resulting bulge or usurpation probably had much to do with the creation of "perspective" painting. For pure visual space is flat, about 180 degrees, while pure acoustic space is spherical. Perspective translated into visual terms the depths of acoustic space. The unscrambling of this mélange occurred via the photograph, which freed painters to return to flat space. Today we are experiencing the emotional and intellectual jag resulting from the rapid translation of varied visual and auditory media into one another's modalities.

THE HOT AND COOL INTERVIEW

With Gerald Emanuel Stearn

*M*arshall McLuhan and I met twice over a period of six weeks and tape-recorded twenty hours of random discussions. Later I transcribed his remarks and my questions and shaped them into a formal interview. In our two meetings, so far as possible, I limited myself to the role of cipher. I never argued a case, nor did I take it upon myself to disagree with what might be regarded as an evasive or incomplete reply.

The following dialogue is arranged in a pattern similar to that of the book's structure [*McLuhan: Hot and Cool. A Critical Symposium*, ed. Gerald E. Stearn, New York: Dial, 1967]—the questions directed at McLuhan follow, roughly, the order of presentation of the material used to demonstrate the evolution of his system of analysis and the range of his critical adversaries. Obviously, McLuhan did not "answer" all of his critics; and his responses are in no way a formal defense of his views. He seemed quite charmed by this method of critical involvement and considered the dialogue not an opportunity to destroy opponents so much as a playful exercise in the development of his own thoughts.

* * *

STEARN: What originally led to your interest in media and the effect of media upon our culture?

McLUHAN: I was gradually made aware of these things by other people—artists, the new anthropological studies. As you become aware of the different modes of experience in other cultures—and watch them transformed by new, Western technologies—it is difficult to avoid observation. It becomes inevitable to assume that what happens to other people and cultures can happen to us. My present interest is an extension of, and derivative of, my literary work. If I could get a team of media students going, I would happily retire back into literary studies. I find media analysis very much more exciting now simply because it affects so many more people. One measure of the importance of anything is: Who is affected by it? In our time, we have devised ways of making the most trivial event affect everybody. One of the consequences of electronic environments is the total involvement of people in people. The Orientals created caste systems as an area of classified immunity.

Here perhaps my own religious faith has some bearing. I think of human charity as a total responsibility of all, for all. Therefore, my energies are directed at far more than mere political or democratic intent. Democracy as a by-product of certain technologies, like literacy and mechanical industry, is not something that I would take very seriously. But democracy as it belongs very profoundly with Christianity is something I take very seriously indeed.

There have been many more religious men than I who have not made even the most faltering steps in this direction. Once I began to move in this direction, I began to see that it had profound religious meaning. I do not think it my job to point this out. For example, the Christian concept of the mystical body—all men as members of the body of Christ—this becomes technologically a fact under electronic conditions. However, I would not try to theologize on the basis of my understanding of technology. I don't have a background in scholastic thought, never having been raised in any Catholic institution. Indeed, I have been bitterly reproached by my Catholic confrères for my lack of scholastic terminology and concepts.

STEARN: When one looks back at your first book, *The Mechanical Bride*, it appears as a strident, moral tract. What is your present attitude toward the *Bride* and how is it related to your more recent interests?

McLUHAN: *Mechanical Bride* is a good example of a book that was completely negated by TV. All the mechanical assumptions of American life have been shifted since TV; it's become an organic cul-

ture. Femininity has moved off the photographic, glamor cake altogether into the all-involving tactile mode. Femininity used to be a
mingling of visual things. Now it's almost entirely nonvisual. I happened to observe it when it was reaching the end of its term, just
before TV.

In 1936, when I arrived at Wisconsin, I confronted classes of
freshmen and I suddenly realized that I was incapable of understanding them. I felt an urgent need to study their popular culture: advertising, games, movies. It was pedagogy, part of my teaching program.
To meet them on their grounds was my strategy in pedagogy: the
world of pop culture. Advertising was a very convenient form of
approach. I used advertising in the *Bride* because of legal considerations—no permissions were needed. Otherwise I would have used
picture stories of any sort from movies, magazines, anywhere. I had
thirty or forty slides and gave little talks to student groups. I invited
them to study these ads. In England, at Cambridge, when I arrived
there, it had become popular to look at films and the popular culture
around us as something to be studied and understood as a "language." Wyndham Lewis did various studies on pop culture. Leavis
has a book called *Culture and Environment.* There was a similar interest in popular speech idioms, language, the *Wake. The Waste Land* is
full of these pop-cult forms. Pound's *Cantos* have similar forms.
Pound has a very useful guide to the *Cantos* called *Kulchur.* In doing
the *Bride* I was merely trailing behind some interesting predecessors.
I discovered that when you take anything out of the daily newspapers
and put it on the screen, people go into a fit of laughter. Like Mort
Sahl. He would take random items from the press and read them out
to an audience straightforwardly. People never notice the outrageous
humor until something is removed from its form. Because it's environmental and invisible. The moment you translate it into another
medium it becomes visible—and hilarious.

Movies on TV are, in a sense, a parody. Just using one form over
another form creates that comic effect. When movies were new it
was suggested that they were a parody of life. The transcript of ordinary visual life into a new medium created hilarious comedy. The
word parody means a road that goes alongside another road. A movie
is a visual track that goes alongside another visual track, creating
complete terror. I did take time to read the language of the form and

discovered that most people couldn't read that visual language. If I merely reprinted ads, without any appended dialogue, the book would have been hilarious in any case. That kind of book ought to be an annual. When you change its environment you flash perception onto it.

In the *Bride* there is far more following of lines of force than simply moral judgments.

Wyndham Lewis was a great influence on me because of his pop-cult analysis. I found Lewis far too moralistic for my tastes. I greatly admired his *method*. Lewis looked at everything as a painter first. His moral judgments never interested me. He was horrified by Bergson and the time philosophy because it seemed to him to destroy various aspects of our Western culture. He said the whole Western culture was based on sight. But he moralized all his life about "ear people" like Bergson who were undermining the visual facets of Western culture. He attacked Spengler in the same way.

Lewis Carroll looked through the looking glass and found a kind of space-time which is the normal mode of electronic man. Before Einstein, Carroll had already entered that very sophisticated universe of Einstein. Each moment, for Carroll, had its own space and its own time. Alice makes her own space and time. Einstein, not Lewis Carroll, thought this was astonishing.

STEARN: Did you learn anything from editing *Explorations* or from your contributors?

McLUHAN: Giedion influenced me profoundly. *Space, Time and Architecture* was one of the great events of my lifetime. Giedion gave us a language for tackling the structural world of architecture and artifacts of many kinds in the ordinary environment. He learned this language from his preceptor, Wölfflin, whose principles of art history revolutionized the entire language of art criticism at the end of the nineteenth and the beginning of the twentieth centuries.

Wölfflin, in turn, had studied with Burckhardt. But Wölfflin was a much abler man than Burckhardt. He moved the European world into a haptic orbit and discovered the structure of various art schools. He approached them not descriptively—not by classification—but structurally. Giedion began to study the environment as a structural, artistic work—he saw language in streets, buildings, the very texture of form.

We started *Explorations* when we felt we had something to say. We stopped it when we felt that we had said it. We decided to write books and free ourselves from the kind of slavery involved in a repetitive operation like publishing a journal. We did discover that readers like a journal that appears on an irregular basis. Most readers of most journals are very unhappy about their regular appearance.

STEARN: Blissett's parody-critique, written in 1957, seems to have anticipated some of the later criticism directed at the *Galaxy* and *Understanding*.

McLUHAN: The complaints about irregular, disconnected, irrational elements in *Explorations* show a complete unawareness. Connected sequential discourse, which is thought of as rational, is really visual. It has nothing to do with reason as such. Reasoning does not occur on single planes or in a continuous, connected fashion. The mind leapfrogs. It puts things together in all sorts of proportions and ratios instantly. To put down thoughts in coded, lineal ways was a discovery of the Greek world. It is not done this way, for example, in the Chinese world. But to deny that the Chinese have access to reason would be ridiculous. They do not have rational discourse at all by Western standards. They reason by the act of interval, not by the act of connection. In the electric age we are moving into a world where not the connection but the interval becomes the crucial event in organization. For people to waste their time lamenting the disappearance of logic and rational, connected discourse when they are really under the illusion that this is actually related to man's reasoning powers is simple non-fact. It is rather sad for people to waste a great deal of energy and moral indignation on things that don't exist, and never have.

On the other hand to say or even suggest that continuous connected discourse is valueless is something I would *never* say. All that I will say is that it isn't rational, it's visual. Why not be accurate? If you're going to order life visually, that is how it is done. Now if you're going to be rational you may have many other ideas about spacing. Once you move into an ear world (for example, the musician moves by interval, not by connection), once you move out of the visual order, you at once discover new modes of rationality. In the electric age we are discovering new modes of rationality. I am not saying this is a "good" thing. I'm simply trying to understand what is happening and how it's done.

All that Blissett is attempting to record here is the sense of lack of connection between events in *Explorations*. The moment you see that the problem is to invent tools—probes—rather than to make continuous (I never saw the parody before today) connected statements, you alarm writers like Blissett. They really think that connected statements are a means of organizing energy and perceptions. They are actually a way of reporting things already seen. You take a statement and turn it around, using it as probe into the environment instead of using it descriptively—as a means of packaging information, already picked up—the idea of using language and statement as probe in this sense just baffles them. On the other hand if they waited around long enough to find out what you were doing they might say, "Oh, why didn't you tell me." It just never dawns on these people, and they're so put off! Their perceptions are so irritated by what they immediately encounter that they never wait around to discover anything. The immediate effect of encountering new forms is, for many people, the cause for scampering back into old ones, where they feel more at home, more comfortable. They are using the language of the consumer, of the person who collects impressions and who is a passive receiver of impressions. This is the language of the dilettante, the amateur, of the fragile, ever so delicate, person. These people put all their energies into dull and conventional materials, second and third rate matters.

Explorations became an international magazine because it had something to say to the world, something new. It excited a lot of people. The idea that one could run something of real international interest and excitement in a backward area like Canada charmed them. Canadians are all a very humble bunch. They take it for granted that everything they do must be second rate. Carpenter and I just blithely assumed that, since nearly everything in the world is second rate at best, there was no reason why we couldn't do something that was first rate right here. So it happened.

STEARN: The anthropologist, Dell Hymes, claims that some of your comparisons go to "ludicrous extremes" and he cites your remarks in the *Galaxy* that "print . . . made bad grammar possible" and: "Nobody ever made a grammatical error in a nonliterate society."

McLUHAN: Obviously he's not talking about native societies. He is talking about illiterate American speech. Natives are bewildered when they hear grammatical errors in their tongue committed by visiting anthropologists who don't know how to speak Urdu or Eskimo. Until anthropologists arrive, the native has never heard a grammatical error in his own tongue. Suppose you made a grammatical error in slang. No child ever made a grammatical error in slang. It would just be funny. Slang is an oral form in which we have infallibility. On the other hand, try to write down slang and everybody is going to make mistakes. Etienne Gilson is fond of using American slang and frequently gets it wrong—"Now we come to zee brass tacks."

One of the more unfortunate features of the entire anthropological enterprise in the twentieth century is that its practitioners are almost entirely and unconsciously literate. They approach structures of nonliterate and oral societies with many of the expectations and patterns which they have acquired from their own highly literate society. Margaret Mead and I have discussed this at some length. She told me of a strange event that occurred in the Admiralty Islands. When she returned there, she had copies of some of her books. Some of the natives noticed that the copies were the same. They got very excited. This was the first time they had seen two books that were alike. They were so excited they said, "They're the same! They're the same!" Now this is an oral, illiterate response to literacy. The idea that you can have the same thing repeated exactly was, to them, a miracle. Now that is a genuine and legitimate response to the printed word. Literary people have never had that response.

The anthropologists of our time have been extremely guilty of importing, uncritically, literate assumptions into nonliterate areas of study; of using models of perception that have no relevance to their materials. These models are constructed of literacy, visual points of view. Anthropologists, for example, assume that vision, as they perceive it in its Western mode, is normal to mankind, that other people see this way too. Anthropologists write about these societies without correcting the bias of their own visual habits. I have been much influenced by anthropology in the sense that I have uncovered material very useful in studying media. Hymes is a very good example of the uncritical, literate anthropologist importing literate assumptions into a nonliterate *world*.

Ted Carpenter has written me about the Hymes critique of the
Galaxy:

Hymes is bluffing. He pretends that much is known about the shifting of
sense ratios by the new extensions of man. The authorities he cites make
no contribution to this subject, nor do anthropologists or linguists
generally. They cannot even be trusted to recognize the significance of
such an approach when they encounter it. Hymes is merely defending
his own unconscious, literate stake in a field he doesn't understand.

Anthropologists see themselves as daring explorers, way out in front.
Most are actually nineteenth century in outlook. They deal with data
atomistically and feel free to abstract them and create regularities for
them. Their visual models are highly ethnocentric, totally ill-suited to
understanding nonliterate patterns. Models offered by Joyce, Klee, and
Pound are ignored. The alienation theme of Man vs. Environment, so dear
to the nineteenth century, survives among them like a watch ticking in the
pocket of a dead man.

Yet anthropologists hold a monopoly on a body of data of prime
importance to the understanding of environments as natural extensions
of man. Their models blind them to the significance of these data;
professionalism prevents them from accepting ideas which threaten
existing management. Hymes' review is a classic example of this
combined blindness and fear.

In objecting to McLuhan's forceful style, Hymes misses the point that
technology is explicitness. Rumors that Al Smith ate peas with a knife
would not have hurt him prior to 1920. Americans didn't become self-
conscious about eating habits until films made these explicit. Remember
the film comedy with eyeglasses equipped with windshield-wipers for
protection while eating grapefruit? Such films are now immensely
popular in Russia.

Language etiquette was linked to print, just as table etiquette was linked
to film. The sudden interest in linguistic decorum during the reign of
James I arose when print made grammar clearly visible. Similarly,
typewriters increased dictionary sales. Bad penmanship could no longer
conceal bad spelling.

The press and typewriter speeded up information flow, creating the
need for more explicit rules of language, just as the motorcar created the
need for more explicit traffic regulations.

It was Western man, not McLuhan, who carried the individualizing
capacity of print, and the lineal nature of the thinking it fosters, to
"ludicrous extremes."

McLuhan suggests that lineal thinking alone is not capable of grasping and understanding our world in a global manner. He offers no single-minded, oversimplified exegesis, but opens the way for multiple models simultaneously applied. One obstacle to such an all-at-once analysis is the single-minded, oversimplified, obsolete approach which Hymes seems to be saying offers "an adequate view of human history."

STEARN: Perhaps the most repeated and passionate dissents emerge from what many critics call your historicism. John Simon's charge—that you play the history of ideas game none too well—has been repeated quite often. You have said that without radio, no Hitler; that the Russians have an "ear" culture and consequently found the U-2 a sensory intruder, not merely the belligerent act of a hostile power.

McLUHAN: The Russians find it unbearable to have "eyes" around their environment. Just as we hate the idea of having "ears" in our own—*vide*: the microphone in the embassy eagle. The Russians live much more by ear than we do. Their new high-rise apartments are at once transformed into villages. All communication between fellow apartment dwellers is like that of a village square. They must live this way. In India, for example, when they tried to put in cold running water, it pulled the village women away from the well. This destroyed community life. They had to remove the pipes. You cannot put running water into an aural community without distressful circumstances.

When you make a structural analysis, you follow lines of force and follow not just one but many, at various levels of the culture, observing patterns. All semiliterate or "backward" cultures are aural cultures, whether it's Ghana or China. They organize space differently, at all times. The Eskimo world is an ear one. When asked to draw maps, they draw areas they've never seen. From their kyacks they've heard water lapping against shores. They map by ear and it later proves quite adequate when checked by aerial photo. Except that there is always an exaggerated area where they've camped. That part receives a stress or bulge in their map. The natural world of non-literate man is structured by the total field of hearing. This is very difficult for literary people to grasp. The hand has no point of view. The ear has no point of view.

Years ago when I was working with Carpenter on anthropological matters, I used acoustic and auditory space frequently as a basic counterploy to visual Western man. I gave it up because I found that the literary people made desperate attempts to visualize auditory space. But you cannot visualize auditory space, that is: a total field of simultaneous relations, without center or margin. Carpenter has remarked that anthropological materials are now beginning to be made up and published by natives themselves—their own stories are being retold by natives themselves. And the results are totally different from what the anthropologists said earlier. We now realize that a nonvisual culture cannot be reported by a visual man.

A prose statement is a reduction to visual terms, like legal language—which is an extreme, unrealistic case of visual organization.

It isn't accidental that the primary arts of Russia are music and ballet. They are not a literary people at all. The world of Dostoevski is not literary. It's a newspaper world, like Edgar Allen Poe or Dickens (an Ann Landers type). This does not contradict the fact that they take literacy far more seriously (and literally) than the West does. Russians, for example, are quite agitated about the telephone.

Russia never had a Renaissance, in terms of space. Realism, perspective art, is avant-garde for them. When you have the means of realistic representation, you also have the means of mechanical production. Mechanical production comes out of visual realism in the Western world. What we think of as realism is to them (Russians) absolute fantasy.

Kafka isn't realism in our world. It's allegorical fantasy (like Bosch). Similarly, Western visual man would have great difficulty in "reading" a tactile piece of information.

To pre-literate man, space was sacred.

A lot of this aural culture is found now in the Negro world. The reason that they are so far ahead of us in the arts is, quite simply, that they haven't trained their visual sense to the point of suppressing the other senses. In music—dance and song—Negroes are ahead.

The generations gap between parents and children is quite simple—children are auditory, nonvisual in their orientation. Teenagers are returning to a backward phase.

All literate cultures sentimentalize all primitive cultures, whether as anthropologists or new neighbors of Negroes. We sentimentalize their primitive state automatically as superior to our own. This confuses a lot of perception, of course.

STEARN: Is the Cold War then merely a sensory conflict?

MCLUHAN: We have a huge cold war going on inside our own borders concerning territorial conflicts, ambitions, jurisdictions, economic demands, etc. These are hugely exaggerated misunderstandings born of sensory divergencies. Our inability to understand them mutually exasperates our negotiations in dealing with them. This exasperation is quite independent of the actual sources of conflict. The same with Castro and dealing with Cuba, with its intensely backward, aural culture. The Cuban way of thinking and feeling about problems is quite alien to our modes of understanding. It's the same with the American Southerner, who has very backward, aural ways of thinking and feeling. It's very hard for the literate North to give him credit for being honest and sincere at all.

De Tocqueville was able to predict certain developments in American culture by contrasting the lack of auditory background in America with its ability to blueprint its development in visual, literate terms. He was making equations. He encountered a new land in which literacy had no opposition, except from Indians. Visual literacy marched unimpeded by any other sensory mode. For the first time in the history of the world, a great new technology encountered a great, new space.

De Tocqueville could not blueprint older, European cultures. But to an ear-oriented European, the American literate culture was quite visible. Mrs. Trollope spoke about auditory, nonvisual factors—which the English even in our time find impossible to deal with. They are unable to realize that they have a class struggle based upon ear culture. We accept literacy and they don't. Literacy wipes out tonality. Americans have never permitted a tone of voice to dictate a man's importance in this world. The English use that criterion entirely as a basis of judging human excellence. In highly literate, visual America it is correct spelling and grammar, not correct intonation. T. S. Eliot lacked an English voice and they did not accept him there. Pound just romped through England wearing a mask of outrageous Yankee dialect. They accepted that. The British are unaware of their auditory culture; we're quite unaware of our visual culture.

STEARN: Similarly, you claim that the war in Vietnam is, more or less, a creature of television.

McLUHAN: Without an informed public there would be no war. We live in an informational environment and war is conducted with information. TV news coverage of Vietnam has been a disaster as far as Washington is concerned because it has alienated people altogether from that war. Newspaper coverage would never alienate people from the war because it's "hot," it doesn't involve. TV does and creates absolute nausea. It's like public hangings—if there were public hangings there would be no hangings. Because public hangings would *involve* people. The distant statistical fact—"At 5:30 this morning so and so was executed"—that's hot. Washington is still fighting a "hot" war, as it were, by newspaper means and the old technologies. The effects of the new technologies on war coverage is not something Washington is prepared to cope with. In Washington people do not concede that the news on TV and news in the press are dissimilar.

TV has begun to dissolve the fabric of American life. All the assumptions—all the ground rules—based on visuality, superficiality, blueprinting, connectedness, equality, sameness—disappear with TV.

STEARN: If you shut off TV, then we would end the war in Vietnam and at the same time set back the civil rights movement?

McLUHAN: Oh yes. But there is an alternative: Put hundreds of extra lines on the TV image, step up its visual intensity to a new hot level. This might serve to reverse the whole effect of TV. It might make the TV image photographic, slick, like movies: hot and detached. Bell Telephone is now operating with eight-thousand-line TV images, not eight hundred, quite beyond the fidelity of any known photographic process.

STEARN: Why hasn't this been tried?

McLUHAN: You might well inquire. No one believes these factors have any effect whatever on our human reactions. It's like the old days when people played around with radium, painting watch dials and they licked the brushes. They didn't believe radium could affect people.

STEARN: George Steiner claims that you have much to tell us about Freud and Marx. Have they influenced you at all?

McLUHAN: Marx's statement should have been: "If you want to change the world, you have to understand it." Freud's notion of ever-increasing repression is simply a remark on the ever-increasing visuality, blueprinting of society. Electronic conditions provided a release from that visuality. I've read Freud and Jung and used them to make discoveries of my own—just as any literary person has been influenced by them. For example, Freud's *Interpretation of Dreams* reveals the amazing power that all people have in their dream life of invention and poetic discovery, that the most ordinary person in his dream life is a tremendous poet. Most Freudians are concerned with the subject matter of this poetry. That never interested me. I was always fascinated by the amazing ingenuity, symmetry, and inventiveness of the dreamer. We all have these tremendous unused powers which we use surreptitiously. We are afraid to use them in our waking lives. Except the artist. The artist uses in his waking life the powers an ordinary person would use in his dream life. The creative man has his dream life while awake. This is the meaning of the title *Finnegans Wake*—mankind is approaching that state of dreaming wide awake. Come Marconi, as environment, dream life became art form. The old romantic dream becomes art form.

Marx was looking in the rear-view mirror of Adam Smith and Ricardo. I'm looking in the rear-view mirror of Joyce, Carroll, the Symbolists, Adolph Hildebrand. They related the sensory life of metamorphosis and transformation in contact with new technology.

STEARN: George Steiner has remarked adversely on your concept of the "global village."

McLUHAN: This is amazing confusion of mind here on the part of Mr. Steiner. There is more diversity, less conformity under a single roof in any family than there is with the thousands of families in the same city. The more you create village conditions, the more discontinuity and division and diversity. The global village absolutely insures maximal disagreement on all points. It never occurred to me that uniformity and tranquillity were the properties of the global village. It has more spite and envy. The spaces and times are pulled out from between people. A world in which people encounter each other in depth all the time.

The tribal-global village is far more divisive—full of fighting—than any nationalism ever was. Village is fission, not fusion, in depth. People leave small towns to *avoid* involvement. The big city *lined* them with its uniformity and impersonal milieu. They sought propriety and in the city, money is made by uniformity and repeatability. Where you have craftsmanlike diversity, you make art, not money. The village is not the place to find ideal peace and harmony. Exact opposite. Nationalism came out of print and provided an extraordinary relief from global village conditions. I don't *approve* of the global village. I say we live in it.

It's like the universe. Margaret Fuller said, "I accept the universe," and Carlyle said, "Yes, you'd better."

I accept media as I accept cosmos. They assume I'm for or against Gutenberg. Bunk! I think of technologies as highly identifiable objects made by our own bodies. They feel that technologies are strange, alien intruders from outer space.

STEARN: When you say that technologies are extensions of man, are they as well extensions of man's will?

McLUHAN: In the ordinary sense of subliminal wish and drive—yes. Man, however, never intends the cultural consequences of any extension of himself.

STEARN: What are we to do with all this information? How does it affect our consciousness?

McLUHAN: When man is overwhelmed by information, he resorts to myth. Myth is inclusive, time-saving, and fast. Children are driven today into mythic thinking. When environmental effects shift beyond a certain point, everybody agrees on a new strategy.

To be conscious or unconscious is to make a certain order of experience. I possess no theory of consciousness. But that says nothing. Throughout my work, however, I am saying that awareness is being pushed more and more out into the environment. Technology pushes human awareness out into the environment. Art becomes environment. Our environments are made of the highest levels of human consciousness.

STEARN: Many readers have been shocked and confused by what they consider idiosyncratic methods in your work. For example: A number of critics suggest that your books are repetitious and, in Dwight Macdonald's words, "ultimately boring."

McLUHAN: Macdonald's is the kind of confusion that comes to the literary mind when confronted with a drilling operation. Repetition is really drilling. When I'm using a probe, I drill. You repeat naturally when you're drilling. But the levels are changing all the time. Macdonald thinks *that's* repetition. There is a complete unawareness of what is going on in the book. His remark that the book might have been an article reveals another fallacy of the literary mind—that the purpose of facts is for classification. The idea of using facts as probes—as means of getting into new territories—is utterly alien to them. They use facts as classified data, as categories, as packages.

Literally, *Understanding Media* is a kit of tools for analysis and perception. It is to *begin* an operation of discovery. It is not the completed work of discovery. It is intended for practical use. Most of my work in the media is like that of a safecracker. In the beginning I don't know what's inside. I just set myself down in front of the problem and begin to work. I grope, I probe, I listen, I test—until the tumblers fall and I'm in. That's the way I work with all these media.

Depth operations are natural to modern studies in all fields including psychiatry and metallurgy and structural analysis. In order to inspect any situation structurally you have to inspect it from all sides simultaneously, which is a sort of cubist gimmick. A structural approach to a medium means studying its total operation, the *milieu* that it creates—the environment that the telephone or radio or movies or the motorcar created. One would learn very little about the motorcar by looking at it simply as a vehicle that carried people hither and thither. Without understanding the city changes, suburban creations, service changes—the environment it created—one would learn very little about the motorcar. The car then has never really been studied structurally, as a form.

If you look at print not as a conveyer belt of data but as a structure somewhat different from the spoken word, somewhat different from manuscript culture, then you are at once in a world where you have to repeat yourself furiously in order to capture all facets simultaneously. The literary form is truly not adapted to simultaneity and structural awareness and this of course is inherent in the very first acts of writing in early times when a vast amount of human awareness was tossed out. Very little of the qualities of speech can be captured by written form, very little of nuance, very little of the drama and action of speech can be captured by written form whatever. But today, with the oscillograph, tape recorder, and various electronic devices, speech is being felt in depth and discovered in structural multi-facet-ness for the first time in human history. So naturally anybody who has become vividly aware of the many, many structural facets of speech, when confronted with the literary form, is aghast at its impoverished character. It's very abstract—it has eliminated most language and speech from its medium. The moment you begin to look at speech as a structure you quickly understand why writing as a structure really cannot deal with much speech. The great poets, starting with Baudelaire and Rimbaud, were quite aware of this and began to substitute all sorts of new literary techniques as a way of capturing the multi-facet-ness of speech. Symbolism discovered that in order to capture the live drama of speech you have to break up the sentence and break up language. That's what Symbolism means—it comes from the Greek *symballein*—to break things into bits and reassemble them into patterns. This was a monetary or economic configuration in the Greek world—break things into single bits and give them out to various parties in a transaction. Symbolism attempted to capture a much larger portion of human speech and language. Anybody who has to have a very thorough initiation into Symbolist art—both painterly and poetic—would not really be in a very good position to look at Gutenberg technology or its rivals in electronic circuitry.

Macdonald (and other literary critics) have never thought for one minute about the book as a medium or a structure and how it related itself to other media as a structure, politically, verbally, and so on. It's not peculiar to Macdonald. It's true of the entire academic world, of the whole journalistic world. They have never studied any medium.

STEARN: Are you an "enemy of the book"? John K. Jessup (in the *Yale Review*) claims that you have "sold the pass of reason and joined the assault on it." Your observations have become infatuations. George P. Elliott says your relationship to the book as "form" appears somewhat ambivalent. Raymond Williams' comment that if one follows your argument—specifically that print culture conditions our mind—then paradoxically, if the book [*The Gutenberg Galaxy*] works, "it to some extent annihilates itself." Have you, after Blake, "become what you behold"?

MCLUHAN: It is customary in conventional literary circles to feel uneasy about the status of the book and of literacy in our society. Macdonald and others, heaven knows, are nineteenth not twentieth-century minds. Therefore anybody who looks at it in a kind of clinical spirit is regarded as hostile, and an enemy of the book.

My own motivation in studying all media began with my commitment to literature as a profession and I quickly became aware that literature had a great many enemies. (They are all of our own making. We have created them.) I discovered that the enemies of literature needed very careful scrutiny and study if the literary man was to manage to extricate himself from this new jungle. So the literary people, I became aware, were so uneasy about the surround of enemies that any attention given to literature as such was considered unfortunate and, as Dwight Macdonald says, "gloomy." And it's a past subjunctive. Any attention to the book is regarded as unfriendly because it is felt that the book will not bear scrutiny any more. Now, in the same way, any attention to new media which are in the ascendant, whose gradient is climbing rapidly, is considered as an act of optimism. Anybody who would direct intellectual attention to a new medium must be an optimist because the rearview look of the nineteenth-century mind in contemplating literature is essentially a pessimistic one. That's why I say "past subjunctive." There are only two cases, you see, in classifying one's relation to almost anything in merely literary terms—you are either "for" or "against." It's as simple as that. So if you write about the book you must be against it because the book is declining in terms of its overall cultural role. If you write about new media in the ascendant, you must be in favor of it. Such is the Western devotion to facts that the mere stating of any case is considered a hostile act. The idea of stating without approval or disapproval is alien to the literary man who finds classification indispensable for order.

STEARN: When Eric Goldman asked you on "The Open Mind" if media change—the electronic revolution of our time, for example—was a "good" or "bad" thing, you replied:

> Now, you see, you have slipped into the literary language of the classifier. The visual man is always trying to check things out by classification and matching.
>
> Goldman: I have set it in the language of the social commentator. You have said something is happening in our society. We now have a medium which is bombarding us, all of our senses.
>
> McLuhan: But when you say "good," is it good in relation to what? You know, the social scientist—
>
> Goldman: Is it good in relation to the established values of the West, let us say?
>
> McLuhan: You remember what the social scientist said to a friend of his: "How is your wife?" And the other social scientist replied, "Do you mean is she better? If so, in relation to what?"

McLUHAN: Classification, for the literary man, is the be-all and end-all of observations. That's why Macdonald attempts to classify me. In the medical world, classification is a form of dismissal. If the doctor says it's measles, that's it, it's over with. The rest is just routine. But classification is not the beginning of the study of a problem—it's the end. For me any of these little gestures I make are all tentative probes. That's why I feel free to make them sound as outrageous or extreme as possible. Until you make it extreme, the probe is not very efficient. Probes, to be effective, must have this edge, strength, pressure. Of course they *sound* very dogmatic. That doesn't mean you are committed to them. You may toss them away.

There is an alternative to classification and that is exploration. This doesn't easily register with nineteenth-century minds. Most nineteenth-century minds are helpless in discussing contemporary forms. They have never acquired the verbal means of grappling with a pictorial world. Macdonald has no verbal strategies for even coping with the movies, let alone more subtle or more recent forms, like radio or television.

I'm perfectly prepared to scrap any statement I ever made about any subject once I find that it isn't getting me into the problem. I have no devotion to any of my probes as if they were sacred opinions. I have no proprietary interest in my ideas and no pride of authorship as such. You have to push any idea to an extreme, you have to probe. Exaggeration, in the sense of hyperbole, is a major artistic device in all modes of art. No painter, no musician ever did anything without extreme exaggeration of a form or a mode, until he had exaggerated those qualities that interested him. Wyndham Lewis said: "Art is the expression of a colossal preference" for certain forms of rhythm, color, pigmentation, and structure. The artist exaggerates fiercely in order to register this preference in some material. You can't build a building without huge exaggeration or preference for a certain kind of space.

This question of repetition bothers them most because they are looking for values or a "point of view." Now values, insofar as they register a preference for a particular kind of effect or quality, are a highly contentious and debatable area in every field of discourse. Nobody in the twentieth century has ever come up with any meaningful definition or discussion of "value." It doesn't work any longer in economics, let alone humanist affairs. It is rather fatuous to insist upon values if you are not prepared to understand how they got there and by what they are now being undermined. The mere moralistic expression of approval or disapproval, preference or detestation, is currently being used in our world as a substitute for observation and a substitute for study. People hope that if they scream loudly enough about "values" then others will mistake them for serious, sensitive souls who have higher and nobler perceptions than ordinary people. Otherwise, why would they be screaming.

Anybody who spends his time screaming about values in our modern world is not a serious character. You might as well start screaming about a house that's burning down, shouting, "This is not the act of a serious man!" When your old world is collapsing and everything is changing at a furious pitch, to start announcing your preferences for old values is not the act of a serious person. This is frivolous, fatuous. If you were to knock on the door of one of these critics and say, "Sir, there are flames leaping out of your roof, your house is burning," under these conditions he would then say to you, "That's a very interesting point of view. I personally couldn't disagree with you more." That's all these critics are saying. Their house is burning and they're saying, "Don't you have any sense of values, simply telling people about fire when you should be thinking about the serious content, the noble works of the mind?" Value is irrelevant.

STEARN: But if "value is irrelevant" what about the *content* of media? In your discussions with Eric Goldman this same point was raised:

> Goldman: Mr. McLuhan, a number of commentators have said that as they understand your view, you really don't think that changing the contents of television would change much about this process. . . .
>
> McLuhan: No. You may have seen a *New Yorker* joke. A couple are watching TV, and one says, "When you think of the vast educational potential of TV, aren't you glad it doesn't?" This is based on the assumption, you see, that it is the content that does the educating, not the medium. Now, if it should be just the other way around—and very few people have asked themselves anything about that—then it would be understandable why these things happen involuntarily and unasked.
>
> Goldman: Take "Peyton Place." If you put on "Peyton Place" or if you put on a news documentary, the contents are radically different in that case, but still from your point of view the medium is transcending the contents in significance so far as the person out there is concerned.
>
> McLuhan: It's like changing the temperature in a room. It doesn't matter what's in the room at all, or what pictures are on the wall, or who is in the room. If the temperature drops forty degrees suddenly, the effect on our outlook, our attitude, is profound.
> Media are like that. They just alter the total social temperature. Since TV, the whole American political temperature has cooled down, down, down, until the political process is almost approaching *rigor mortis.* These facts of media are not the areas in which they look—after all, the medical profession was in the habit of looking in the wrong places for causes and effects for many centuries, and nobody has come up with any suggestions for how to control media or the social impact of technologies until now.

McLUHAN: Many people would rather be villains than nitwits. It occurs to me just now that moral vehemence may provide ersatz dignity for our normal moronic behavior. It would be possible to extend my media analysis to include the idea that the normal human condition, when faced with innovation, is that of the brain-washed idiot who tries to introduce the painfully learned responses from one situ-

ation into new situations where they apply not at all. The reason that
I refrain in the book from pointing out this obvious moral is owing to
the discovery, represented by the book itself, that this helpless and
witless condition of persistent irrelevance of response is unnecessary
at the first moment that we recognize this pattern of response and its
causes. It is this discovery that fills me with optimism. The moralist
has instinctively translated my forward-looking discovery into back-
ward-looking misanthropy. Moral bitterness is a basic technique for
endowing the idiot with dignity. Guilt and remorse are retrospective
by definition and exempt the guilty party from any redeeming act of
expiation or creative renewal. Guilt and remorse are forms of despair
and sloth. Any charge of nonmoral fervor with regard to my work
merely points to my own effort to protect reader and critic from the
rage and indignation which they have richly earned. For many years
I have observed that the moralist typically substitutes anger for perception. He hopes that many people will mistake his irritation for
insight. Is this not one of the great attractions of Marxism? While
lacking all insight into the processes with which it is concerned, it yet
provides an intensely dramatic role for the corporate expression of
dissatisfactions that elude the understanding.

Do I "approve of 'Peyton Place' or of Jack Paar"? No! But
they're trying to classify Paar with a good or bad "thing," not
attempting to find out *what* he's doing or what effect he's having or
what's really going on. They are trying to fit him into some sort of
encyclopedia of culture. They find *concept* a much more convenient
form of human activity than *percept*. They ask me to judge what I
observe. Cocteau said: "I don't want to be famous. I just want to be
believed." Any artist would say that he doesn't want people to agree
or disagree with him. He just wants them to notice. I expect my audience to participate with me in a common act of exploration. I want
observations, not agreement. And my own observation of our almost
overwhelming cultural gradient toward the primitive—or involvement of all the senses—is attended by complete personal distaste and
dissatisfaction. I have no liking for it.

Since, however, this new cultural gradient is the world, the
milieu, in which I must live and which prepares the students I must
teach, I have every motive to understand its constituents, its components, and its operations. I move around through these elements as I

hope any scientist would through a world of disease and stress and misery. If a doctor, surgeon or scientist were to become personally agitated about any phenomenon whatever, he would be finished as an explorer or observer. The need to retain an attitude of complete clinical detachment is necessary for survival in this kind of work. It is not an expression of approval or a point of view or outlook. It's only a strategy of survival. Anybody who enters this kind of work with strong feelings of approval or disapproval, nineteenth-century-style point of view, fixed positions, "From where I'm sitting I would say that this is an abomination and degradation of all human values," etc.—anybody who enters any situation in our time with any such commitments has completely polished himself off the scene as an observer. He's had it. So our literary fraternities—nineteenth-century liberals if you like—are completely helpless to even approach the material of their own culture. They are so terrified, so revolted, they don't even know how to get near it and they've never bothered to acquire the means of studying or of observing it.

This so-called primitivism—and it is so fatuous in our time, so uncritical—one of the more ridiculous aspects of Picasso, if you like—it's a form of surfboarding, just riding any old wave that happens to be around. On the other hand, primitivism, D. H. Lawrence style, has become in itself almost a form of *camp*. That is why we have suddenly abandoned it in favor of *camp*, which is a new artistic attitude toward our own junkyard. The sudden resolve to tackle our own junkyard as art work is a hopeful indication that we are prepared after all to look at the environment as that which is capable of formulation, patterning, shaping. It still lacks the awareness of what effects environments have upon us. They still seem to imagine that you can take it or leave it. You know the old literate attitude toward advertising in the thirties: "Personally, I can take it or leave it. I'm just not interested in it." These are the helpless victims of all advertising, these people who think that merely by subjecting themselves to it without taking an interest in it they can be immune. The idea of immunity from environments and environments created by media—so long as one concentrates upon noble content—is a cherished illusion in literary circles. I heard a Tom Swiftie the other day—" 'Don't talk to me of icebergs,' said the captain of the *Titanic* sanctimoniously." The literary professions are somewhat in that position. There are many who imagine that we can disregard these forms and their operations on human sensibilities.

Similarly, there are those who feel they can expose themselves to a hideous urban environment so long as they feel they are in a state of literary grace, as it were; that the forms of life are not in themselves communicative; that only classified data register in our apparatus. People would never dream of valuing their daily experiences in terms of what they happen to see or hear *that* day. Media like print or radio or television—which are much more environmental and pervasive forms assailing their eyes and ears all day long—these are invisible. It was only in the nineteenth century that artists, painters, and poets began to notice that it was the environmental form itself, as humanly constituted, that really provided people with the models of perception that governed their thoughts. The literary people still cherish the idea that we can fight off the sensory models imposed on our sensorium by environment, by content, by the classifiable part of the environment. It's somewhat the predicament that Malraux sees in his museum without walls. As long as you can see art inside a museum you can, as it were, protect it from all sorts of vulgarity. What happens when photoengraving and various new technologies make it possible to have far more art *outside* walls of museums than *inside*? How do you maintain taste and artistic standards when you can vulgarize the greatest art with an environment? These are the problems assailing the literary world but which have never been looked into by literary people, journalists, and reviewers.

As a person committed to literature and the literary tradition, I have studied these new environments which threaten to dissolve the whole of literary modality, the whole traditions of literary achievement, and I don't think that these are merely threats to classifiable literary values that can be fended off by staunch moralism or lively indignation. We have to discover new patterns of action, new strategies of survival.

This is where William Burroughs comes in with his *Naked Lunch*. When we invent a new technology, we become cannibals. We eat ourselves alive since these technologies are merely extensions of ourselves. The new environment shaped by electric technology is a cannibalistic one that eats people. To survive one must study the habits of cannibals.

STEARN: Why are some critics so outraged by your work?

McLUHAN: Any new demand on human perception, any new pressure to restructure the habits of perception, is the occasion for outraged response. Literary people prefer to deal with their world without disturbance to their perceptual life. In the sixteenth century, when new forms of perception came into existence with things like printing, people underwent terrified responses as recorded by Hieronymous Bosch. The world of Bosch shows space—the old familiar, comfortable, sensible space of all right-thinking people—medieval, iconic, discontinuous. Against that space he juxtaposes the new world of perspective and three-dimensional space with its strange vanishing point and continuum. By putting these two spaces together he gets the "Temptation of St. Anthony." Quite similarly, Kafka takes the plausible, reasonable, literary modes of discourse and narrative and immediately juxtaposes them with something else—creating metamorphosis, change of structure, change of perception. By putting the three-dimensional world against the metamorphic world of changed structure he gets the same degree of nightmare and terror that Bosch got by putting his two spaces together. Now Bosch was merely recording a response of his age to the experience of pictorial space. To the world of the sixteenth century, rational, three-dimensional, pictorial space was a world of absolute horror. There is no literary horror in the presence of mass culture that could match the horror which the sixteenth century felt in the presence of three-dimensional, rational space. To them it was absolute disaster, absolute spiritual disruption. In our time the plunge through the looking glass of Lewis Carroll into the discontinuous, space-time world of electric technology has created the same sense of the plunge into the abyss, the plunge into the irrational on the part of our contemporaries that we associate with existentialism. Our contemporaries are mistaken, in many ways, as to the causes of their present discontent. On the other hand, they are not mistaken about the demands on their sensibilities and on their perceptions. To shift out of a nineteenth-century, rational space into a twentieth-century space-time, noncontinuum is an experience of great discomfort because it puts one's whole sensorium under terrible pressure.

STEARN: "The communications expert," one of your detractors has remarked, "cannot communicate," underlining Jonathan Miller's observation: "McLuhan opens many doors, including the doors of chaos."

McLUHAN: Communication, in the conventional sense, is difficult under any conditions. People prefer *rapport* through smoking or drinking together. There is more communication there than there ever is by verbal means. We can share environments, we can share weather, we can share all sorts of cultural factors together but communication takes place only inadequately and is very seldom understood. For anybody to complain about lack of communication seems a bit naïve. It's actually very rare in human affairs. This has been studied in our time by F. C. Bartlett in his book *Remembering* or I. A. Richards, and others. The most skilled students of poetry, when their reading and understanding of a poem are checked, are found to be monstrously mistaken. It isn't only country bumpkins who have difficulty reading good poems—it is the professors of literature. They too have a very inadequate relation to the world of poetry and prose. Practical criticism created a mortal terror in the academic world in 1929 because it revealed that the best students and professors were quite incapable of reading ordinary poems.

There is a kind of illusion in the world we live in that communications is something that happens all the time, that it's normal. And when it doesn't happen, this is horrendous. Actually, communication is an exceedingly difficult activity. In the sense of a mere point-to-point correspondence between what is said, done, and thought and felt between people—this is the rarest thing in the world. If there is the slightest tangential area of touch, agreement, and so on among people, *that* is communication in a big way. The idea of complete identity is unthinkable. Most people have the idea of communication as something matching between what is said and what is understood. In actual fact, communication is *making*. The person who sees or heeds or hears is engaged in making a response to a situation which is mostly of his own fictional invention. What these critics reveal is that the mystery of communication is the art of making. What they make in difficulties, confusions, vague responses is natural. It goes on all the time in all human affairs as between parents and children, for example. We are always improvising interpretations of everything we do, see, feel, and hear. With ingenuity, with great skill, we improvise responses in order to enable us to continue our relations with our fellows.

Platonic dialogues come out of an oral rather than a literary culture. In a highly literate culture, the dialogue form becomes repugnant. It came back with radio and panel shows. Highly literate people speak on one level, in a monotone. "Good" prose is spoken this way. A level of form, one plane. You cannot discuss multi-relationships on a single plane, in a single form. That's why the poets of our time have broken all the planes and sequences, forming a cubist prose. "I don't follow you"—as if that had anything to do with reasoning. It has to do with lineality and visuality. Logical or connected discourse is highly visual and has very little to do with human reasoning.

STEARN: If you consider your prose an art form, then your books might be considered as extensions of McLuhan, poetical or artistic outbursts having nothing to do with media?

McLUHAN: The "suggestion" is delightful and far too flattering, based, I think, on an almost ethereal whimsy. But it implies that I have used media analysis as a means of private self-expression. Of course when you talk back to the environment you begin to use it as a means of self-expression. However, I am antienvironment. I am not in awe of media or their contents. For example: When you talk back to ads as I did in *The Mechanical Bride*, they become your servants. Since you cannot survive the effects of media if you huddle or hide, you must rush out and kick them in the guts—give them what for—right in the midriff. And they respond very well to this treatment. Media, after all, are only extensions of ourselves. The road to understanding media effects begins with arrogant superiority. If one lacked this sense of superiority—this detachment—it would be quite impossible to write about them. It would be like an octopus attacking the great pyramids.

The propriety of Mandarin prose, the mask of the upper-middle-class Mandarin world, is simply ludicrous. In *Beyond the Fringe*, when the cast wanted to appear superbly ludicrous, they put on that mask. It is a comic mask, good only for laughs. I can speak "slight" Mandarin prose any time, without effort at all. What we call "acceptable prose" moves along on a single plane while puns do not. When you are dealing with a variety of facets simultaneously, you cannot use that kind of prose. I'm talking that kind of prose right now. The kind Miller thinks I cannot write. I talk it all day long in the classroom. I don't use slang, puns—I use Mandarin prose, the only form of discourse I employ. But when I sit down to write about complicated problems moving on several planes, I deliberately move into multi-level prose. This is an art form. The prose that he's complaining about I consider a serious art form. The prose he considers perfectly natural and conventionally acceptable is a kind of prose that comes in with a high visual cultivation and disappears with aural culture.

In the sense that these media are extensions of ourselves—of man—then my interest in them is utterly humanistic. All these technologies and the mechanisms they create are profoundly human. What does one say to people who cannot see extensions of their own bodies and faculties, who find their environments invisible? They call these same environments alien, nonhuman and search for a "point of view." This is simply the inability to observe ordinary data. Content analysis divorces them from reality.

They are talking about art as a blood bank, as stored precious moments of experience. The idea that art's job is to *explore* experience too never dawned on them. The job of art is not to store moments of experience but to explore environments that are otherwise invisible. Art is not a retrieval system of precious moments of past cultures. Art has a live, on-going function. Milton's phrase—"A great book is the precious life-blood of the master spirit." The humanist fault, since the Renaissance, has been to sell art totally short. Since Gutenberg, art has become a retrieval system. Before, art was a means of merging with the cosmos. My critics' notion of art is incredibly defective and feeble. Blake regarded art as exploratory. He thought of it as a means of uniting all the human faculties, aspiring to the unity of the imagination. Art-as-probe is survival. They are saying: "Without art, what impoverished lives we would lead."

Programmers of computers are still using the old print technology—storage. Computers are being asked to do things that belong to the old technology. The real job of the computer is *not* retrieval but discovery. Like the human memory, the process of recall is an act of discovery.

The dream is a way of processing waking experiences in a pattern which is nonlineal, but multi-leveled. Freud is very literary. His technique of analyzing and presenting his material is elegantly literary. And this is why he is the darling of literary men. Jung is much less literary, much less lineal, much more auditory.

STEARN: Do you *personally* enjoy Jack Paar?

McLUHAN: I've only looked at Paar to try to understand TV. I would never dream of looking at Paar for entertainment. I look at advertising in much the same way. I find it diverting.

I use Jack Paar or any successful practitioner of the art of a particular medium as an instrument of observation. I use them as probes. I'm concerned with Paar's content because that belongs to the old medium. Movies used the gramophone. Books used old manuscripts. This is inevitable. The fact that any new medium must use the old medium as content does not raise the factor of values at all. Questions of value should have been raised when that content was new. We do not measure the success or meaning of any particular day of our lives by the things we have said or seen. The actual use of our faculties day by day is never considered. But we do consider it a great advantage to be able to use our eyes, ears, etc. This is the way we use media—as extensions. Therefore it doesn't matter what's on, what matters is that we have use of our faculties. I'm quite prepared to live the life of Confucius or Plato, day in, day out, in my conversations.

Most media, though, are pure poison—TV, for example, has all the effects of LSD. I don't think we should allow this to happen.

I don't think these literary critics are serious. I don't think they're honest. They don't insist on high standards in the daily life use of their faculties. It is only when they see poor content in some old medium that the question arises. If anyone tried to value painting by the subject matter he would be in a very poor position. Years ago, before I wrote the *Bride*, I had a moralistic approach to all environmental facts. I abominated machinery, cities, everything except the most Rousseauistic. Gradually, I became aware of how useless this was and I discovered that artists of the twentieth-century had a different approach and I adopted it.

STEARN: Frank Kermode quoted a letter of yours to the effect that *The Gutenberg Galaxy* might have been expressed as an ideogram and that you are very much concerned with your own problems of communication.

McLUHAN: I'm trying to get my audience involved in perceptions. So I use their language. The language of their environment.

The idea that the *Galaxy* might have been presented as an ideogram is true. That's the very form it is in. It could also be expressed as a Happening. The word "galaxy" really expresses the simultaneous interplay of factors that are not directly connected at all. It is this pattern of interplay that is both the essence of the electronic speed-up and also the antithesis of the old mechanical connectedness which passed for rationality for centuries.

The literary quotations I use in the *Galaxy* are not intended as footnotes or as part of my argument. They are there as heuristic probes. I could substitute for any one of those quotes twenty or thirty other citations.

The mosaic is a world of intervals in which maximal energy is transferred across the gaps. This is the "massage" effect. *The Gutenberg Galaxy* is a world in which energy is generated in the intervals, not by the connections. And the massage—the shaping, the twisting, the bending of the whole human environment by the technology—the reconditioning of the entire human environment by this technology—is a violent process, like all new technologies often revolting, as well as revolutionary. That is why Joyce calls them "thunders." All revolutionary events are nauseating.

I personally find very little joy in the effects of media. The only satisfaction I derive is learning how they operate. This is cool, in that it is at once involvement and detachment.

I expect my readers to do more work than I did. But I'm offering them opportunities, roles of initiative. When people approached T. S. Eliot and said, "Mr. Eliot, when you were writing 'Sweeney Among the Nightingales' in that passage XYZ did you mean . . ." he would wait patiently and say, "Yes. I must have meant that, if that's what you got out of it." Now Eliot was saying that the reader was co-poet. The reader's job was to make poems. Not to get his essence but to make a poem with the ingredients handed to him. This shocked literary people. That a poet would say, as Eliot did, "I never thought of that but I must have meant it if you got that out of it." That's the way I feel about critical responses. Many of the meanings people get—in so far as they are related to media—are not the ones I had in mind but they might serve very well as exploratory devices. When critics say, "One gets a lot of misconceptions and misunderstandings from these pages," they're being naïve. Not to understand the media of discourse is naïve. What sort of people am I dealing with? Isn't this the kind of image that the Europeans have always had of Americans—naïve, superficial? They are betraying enormous naïveté here. After all when I mark themes of graduate students, I expect naïveté there. And I'm not surprised when I find it in the pages of various American journals. They're no better than the ordinary graduate student.

STEARN: Some critics have argued that "hot and cool" are artificial polarities which permit you to build a system of analysis that fits your whimsy, not your evidence.

MCLUHAN: Perhaps I should have set up polarities on media rigid and frigid. It's very difficult to have a structure of any sort without polarities, without tension. For example, the triangle is the most economical way of securing an upright object. Without polarities, without contraries—this is Blake's whole notion of hateful contraries—without polarities, there is no progression, no structure. For a literary person who likes things to move along in one direction on one plane, polarities are distressing. I must know how media are structured to discover what they are doing, to me and my environment. *Media, hot* and *cool* are not classifications. They are structural forms. These are slang terms from the musical world where they have high, structural meaning. "System" means something to look at. You must have a very high visual gradient to have systemization. In philosophy, before Descartes, there was no "system." Plato had no "system." Aristotle had no "system." My own interest in studying media is a "systems development" approach. "Systems development" is a structural analysis of pressures and strains, the exact opposite of everything that has been meant by "systems" in the past few centuries. "Systems development" is the opposite of "systems" in the philosophical sense. It is concerned with the inner dynamics of the form.

A system has almost entirely visual connotations—as with Newton. The great difficulty of approaching the space-time world, after the Newtonian intrusion, is that one is deprived of visual means of fitting things in. In Newton's world, you fit things into the world. The environment is thought of as a wraparound space into which things are placed like pictorial painting or perspective art. Prior to perspective paintings, each object made its own space (for example, the flat Byzantine world). With the coming of perspective, things began to press down. They had a thrust, a weight. A man's system is thought of as a kind of space into which he puts or arranges his experience. This is the old, visual pattern. Critics are looking for the space into which I fit my experiences. There is no such space.

There is no continuum except that which we impose on things. The only sense which has the effect of continuum is the visual sense. The world of the nineteenth-century dance floor—the ballroom— was a continuum. The world of the twentieth-century dance floor is a discontinuum—a Discothèque à Go-Go, in which a dancer makes his or her own space which does not fit into anybody else's space. It's like a physicist trying to encounter electronic particles with Newtonian concepts.

STEARN: You have been accused of having a philistine enthusiasm for devices, the machines of civilization. The corollary of this charge, of course, being that you are indifferent to man. Christopher Ricks, among others, questions your definition of work. In *Understanding Media* you said: "What the nineteenth century had delegated to servants and housemaids, we now do for ourselves." Switching on a washing machine and actually scrubbing are not considered similar in terms of "work."

McLUHAN: Ricks doesn't consider that his wife's devotion to that electric washing machine is a meaningful substitution for the "navvy" or washerwoman of the nineteenth century. He assigns his wife cheerfully to the role of charwoman and feels himself quite superior to the whole operation. Electric media, for example, create learning for everybody instead of assigning it to specialists. They create an environment of knowledge. Just as work becomes diffused through the total population with electric devices, so does learning. Where learning before had been locked up in little, citational cells and classified slots, under electric conditions all that had been previously cherished, precious, erudite now becomes general, mass-oriented, diffuse—environments. What had previously been the content of a select environment becomes an environment itself. Work becomes an environment. Knowledge, learning become an environment of toil. That is the future work of mankind—just processing the data of the electronic environment. "Labor-saving" is a nineteenth-century concept of work. Jacques Ellul says that the twentieth-century child works harder than any child in human history. What is he working at? Just data processing.

Elizabeth Hardwick told me that in New England toilet-training was abandoned upon the discovery of the electric washing machine. Moral responsibility was shifted to the washing machine.

STEARN: When you speak about environment aren't you actually making value judgments or, at least, content analysis? For example, your much-quoted statement that the space program makes the earth seem like a used nose-cone.

McLUHAN: The safety car—I always like to talk about things which are to me puzzles—is in a certain degree, the death sentence of the existing motorcar. Just as much as the motorcar was the death sentence of the horse and buggy. The motorcar's environment creates roads and surfaces. It doesn't simply occupy a space. It creates its own space. The safety car is a bump car. It will create a totally different environment. When things began to happen all at once, people began to notice the effects of cars. They began to notice what cars do to people. All our technologies in the Western world are built on the assumption that they have complete immunity from inspection. You inspect their content—the old one, not the new one. When you look at the car in terms of what it does to people, it becomes a horrifying story—as bad as the death camps. People were unable to see the road system that came with the car. It was one thing to put the car in the old environment—horse and buggy, old mud roads.

People are now aware of consequences because of electronic information. Why are people suddenly unhappy with capital punishment? Why are they suddenly aware that crime is not committed by private individuals but by the whole society? Now the satellite or space capsule world is only possible as a result of intense study of consequences. This is a new stress in our time. To build a capsule you must foresee all the possible effects on the human form. Buckminster Fuller has remarked that the space capsule is the first completely designed human environment. Up to the present, we have not been designing environments. We have been designing things to put into the environment. It's like finding the right picture for the right room. Now one says, "What kind of a room will grow out of this picture?" The space capsule is an extension of the planet. The safety car is not an event; it's a Happening.

STEARN: Is it possible that self-appointed disciples will somehow distort your work? Are you a McLuhanite?

McLUHAN: You can be quite sure that if there are going to be McLuhanites, I am not going to be one of them. I know that anyone who learns anything will learn it slightly askew. I can imagine that having disciples would become a very great bother. It would disturb one's freedom, privacy, work. If I just keep writing with great energy, no McLuhanite will ever be able to digest it all. My areas of probing, of exploring are very personal. But of course my work might produce considerable consequences for other people. Most of what I have to say is secondhand, gathered however from esoteric sources. My favorite stomping grounds are areas that very few people have ever stomped.

STEARN: Is there a real danger in the new media?

McLUHAN: It seems to me that the great advantage in understanding the operational dynamics of various media is to quiet them down, not exploit them. If you understand these dynamics, you can control media, eliminate their effects from the environment. And this is most desirable. I think we would do ourselves a considerable kindness if we closed down TV operations for a few years. If TV was simply eliminated from the United States scene, it would be a very good thing. Just as radio has a most malignant effect in Africa or Algeria, or China—in highly auditory cultures, radio drives these people nearly mad with paranoia and tribal intensity—TV, in a highly visual culture, drives us inward in depth into a totally nonvisual universe of involvement. It is destroying our entire political, educational, social, institutional life. TV will dissolve the entire fabric of society in a short time. If you understood its dynamics, you would choose to eliminate it as soon as possible. TV changes the sensory and psychic life. It is an oriental form of experience, giving people a somber, profound sense of involvement.

STEARN: When an admirer called him a poet, Freud considered the judgment harmful in that it took away from his scientific intent. A Canadian writer suggests that you are not literary critic, sociologist, historian, or whatever, but, simply, a poet.

McLUHAN: All poets have to probe to discover anything. In our world, there is so much to discover.

STEARN: Can we excuse methodological lapses in the name of poetic and/or artistic license?

McLUHAN: Our sensory modes are constituents, not classifications. I am simply identifying modes of experience. We need new perceptions to cope. Our technologies are generations ahead of our thinking. If you even begin to think about these new technologies you appear as a poet because you are dealing with the present as the future. That is my technique. Most people look back for security. Much greater perceptions and energies are needed than simply mine in the world in which we exist. Better developed talents are needed. James Joyce had these talents in a much more refined state. Joyce had a complete ecology of manmade environments which these critics should have read and studied long ago.

STEARN: Will there ever be silence?

McLUHAN: Objects are unobservable. Only relationships among objects are observable.

STEARN: Are you disturbed by the sometimes harsh critical responses your work excites?

McLUHAN: Even Hercules had to clean the Augean stables but once!

Professor McLuhan in his office at St. Michael's College,
University of Toronto, 1963.

"Everybody experiences far more than he understands. Yet it is experience, rather than understanding, that influences behavior." [a]

ROBERT YARBER
Signal Behavior, 1992
(Courtesy Sonnabend Gallery, New York)

"T he content of speech
is mental dance,
nonverbal ESP." [b]
Consciousness as
dial tone with many
area codes:
smell = present
taste = quality
hearing = receiving
touch = action
sight = territories.

ORNETTE COLEMAN
& PRIME TIME
Tone Dialing, 1995
(Courtesy Harmolodic Inc.)

"I f it is asked, 'What is the
content of speech?,' it is
necessary to say, 'It is an
actual process of thought,
which is in itself nonverbal.' An abstract painting
represents direct manifestation of creative thought
processes as they might
appear in computer
designs.... As informa-
tion becomes our
environment, it becomes
mandatory to program
the environment itself as
a work of art." [c]

DAVID URBAN
Reform School, 1994
(Collection Mr. Ernst Nijkerk, Amsterdam.
Courtesy Galerie Barbara Farber, Amsterdam)

SEE FARTHER.

See into the nation's schoolrooms (the Education page—every Wednesday), courtrooms (the Law page—every Friday), the local and national issues affecting our lives every day in the pages of

𝔗𝔥𝔢 𝔑𝔢𝔴 𝔜𝔬𝔯𝔨 𝔗𝔦𝔪𝔢𝔰

he technological format of *The New York Times* is far more significant than any single report it could ever print. Its well known motto, 'All the news that's fit to print,' could very well be the text for any comic show. Editorial policy is of minute effect compared to the art form of the page itself.... The modern newspaper page is not a mere extension of the book page because the speed with which the telegraph feeds news to the press today precludes any possibility of organizing a sheet of news by any but the most impressionistic devices. Each item lives in its own kind of space totally discontinuous from all other items.

"Literary lenses" or Alice's "looking glass"? "Light *on*" or "light *through*"? "Public" or "Mass"? The newspaper is pivotal hybrid medium for our time, since with the telegraph the press became a mass medium in prototype, the world of global press coverage instituting what was virtually a real-time hyper*text* community, much as now "CNN epitomizes an emerging electronic life-form that is slowly becoming the eyes and ears of the world community." [d]

"*C*alling all daynes. Calling all daynes to down. The old breeding bradsted culminwilth of natures. . . . We have highest gratifications in announcing to pewtewr publikumst of pratician pratyusers, genghis is goon for you."

At the conclusion of *Finnegans Wake* Joyce thus introduces as radio announcers the angelic voices convening the guardians of the new aeon:

"Calling all downs. Calling all downs to dayne. Array! Surrection."

"Calling all cars" of the police radio refers us to the laws of nature which control the process of the aeon or world cycle. The cycle cops or laws of the new cycle are summoned to descend.

A central episode of *Finnegans Wake* presents a long radio and TV broadcast which foreshadows the above radio announcement of the new epoch of world history. The patrons of the pub are enjoying a radio broadcast of news, weather, sports, and drama when their attention is drawn to a mezzotint picture on the wall. It appears to be both the view of the hunt or tallyho story and a picture of the famous Charge of the Light Brigade. As a hunting scene the picture presents red-coated figures bowling along over the green. (Throughout *Finnegans Wake* the drama of oral speech is represented with reference to earwigs on the green.) But as a battle scene the mezzotint of the charge at Balaclava merges into "the bairdboard bombardment screen . . . tends to teleframe and step up to the charge of a light barricade . . . glitteraglatteraglutt, borne by their carnier walve. Spraygun rakes and splits them from a double focus. . . ."

In a word, Joyce saw TV as the fateful charge of the Light Brigade made possible by the "abnihilisation of the etym."

Joyce was the artist of this century who gave the most careful attention to the impact on language and art of all technical development in the means of communication. *Finnegans Wake* is a dramatization of every event known to archaeologists, anthropologists, and physical scientists which concerns the development of oral speech, inner speech, writing, and writing as the direct means of physical and social architecture—walls, cities, families and societies, myths and religions.

There is no logical place to begin the discussion of so protean and inclusive an artist as Joyce who spoke of his sentences as an everyway roundabout with intrusions from above and below. Karl Deutsch is footnoting Joyce's mezzotint of Tallyho and Balaclava when he remarks in *Nationalism and Social Communication*:

, "As spaced dots of animal footprints, patterns of information were the basis of primitive hunting and tracking. As varied electric impulses, patterns of information are today the basis of modern telegraphy, electronics, and automatic equipment. As patterns of sound, sight, or action, they have always been the basis of signaling, of language, of society, of culture."

It is no accident in *Finnegans Wake* that the radio broadcast precedes the TV show. Everywhere in his work Joyce follows the classical philosophical principle that during "the whole of previous time wherein anything is moving towards its form, it is under the opposite form." Silent pictures preceded and prepared the form of talkies, as radio pioneered TV, so the ear readied the eye.

Throughout *Finnegans Wake* Joyce sends telegraph messages to the "abced-minded." That is, to the sleepers locked up in what he calls the nightmare of history, he tries to get through by a sort of telegraphic séance method. But, paradoxically, the abced-minded are the literate. Just as speech is a sort of stacatto stutter or static in the flow of thought, letters are a form of static or oral speech. And letters, requiring as they do translation into inner speech, set up a complex group of mechanical operations between eye and ear which cause physical withdrawal. So to be abced-minded is to be part of the dream of history that is *Finnegans Wake*.

On the relations between earliest writing and telegraph Joyce comments à la Sherlock Holmes:

"The unmistakable identity of the persons in the Tiberiast duplex came to light in the most devious of ways. The original document was in what is known as Hanno O'NonHano's unbrookable script, that is to say, it showed no signs of punctuation of any sort. Yet on holding the verso against a lit rush this new book of Morses responded most remarkably to the silent query of our world's oldest light and its recto let out the piquant fact that it was pierced but not punctured (in the university sense of the term) by numerous stabs and foliated gashes made by a pronged instrument. These paper wounds, four in type, were gradually and correctly understood to mean stop, please stop, do please stop, and O do please stop respectively. . . ."

As Joyce remarks elsewhere, there's "no police like Holmes." His puns are always revelations or epiphanies, as here, in referring to the oldest writing and the newest writing as "this new book of Morse"—the tablets of Moses and the stutter of Morse, each opening up a new world. And as Moses was a stutterer, Morse was a painter. The telegraphic message finally deciphered turns out to be reMorse, "O do please stop."

The relation of the impressionism of Joyce's *Ulysses* to the art of the movie has been discussed by Harry Levin. *Ulysses* is epic in mode and the movie easily lends itself to the panoramic social inclusiveness of epic action. It has become one of the commonplaces of discussion of the TV mode of communication to mention its intimacy. It is clear that TV differs from the movie image both in mode of shooting and projection. TV deals with the visual image as radio with the auditory image. That is, there is immediacy or instantaneity of pick-up, projection, and reception. Joyce was entirely aware of these differences in choosing TV as the basic modality of the collective human drama of *Finnegans Wake*. As immediate sight plus sound, TV permits a full use of the plenary materials of the human drama, namely speech itself, a "verbivocovisual presentment." Paul Elmer More said:

"Language is the medium by which we undertake to convey experience completely and directly rather than as divided and refracted by a particular organ of perception; it may be less intense and precise than the various senses in their proper fields, but is deeper and broader than any one of them."

The movie with its still shots is able to roll up the external daylight world on its reel which can eventually be unreeled in the Platonic cave of the theatre. The movie gives us the day world as night dream. TV is more flexible in being able to give us day or night worlds as night or day. But with TV the spectator is the screen. The world external to the TV camera is interiorized in the TV watcher, as the auditory world, exterior to the microphone, is interiorized directly in us. The movie in its very format encourages the collective dream of the group audience, for the imagery is visibly external as it spumes from the back of the theatre upon the screen. But the "charge of the light barricade"—the direct invasion of the human subject by TV electrons—is an affair of more complex drama. If the movie is Platonic, TV would seem to be Aristotelian in the direct spume of species from things into our inner senses: "Raday to embrace our ruddy inflamttry world . . . till they've kinks in their tringers and boils on their taws. . . . Sing in the chorias to the ethur. . . ." There is often an ominous note, as here, in Joyce's presentment of the new media. It is as though the *flammantia moenia mundi*, the flaming ramparts of outer space had now embraced the psyche of mankind with his acceptance of the electronic "charge of the light barricade." Elsewhere Joyce comments on the human combustion of the Phoenix (Feenichts), playhouse of history, alluding both to *Macbeth* and to the new media of film and radio:

"For a burning would is come to dance inane. Glamours hath moidered's lieb and herefore Coldours must leap no more. Lack breath must leap no more."

Paul Schrecker notes that "work, in the field of language begins when a content of consciousness urging expression is unable to avail itself of petrified and completely specific linguistic clichés." From this point of view Joyce was the Hercules of language labours. He not only, in accordance with changed conditions of technological culture, initiated more new modes of expression than anybody else, but he cleansed the Augean stables of accumulated cliché with the great communal river of words and rhythms which he diverted through the night world of Western consciousness.

Paul Schrecker adds a comment on work and language which will console the Joyce reader: "Now, the same conditions which qualify the production of speech . . . invest the understanding of speech with the same potentiality." The reader of Joyce has to exert as much precision of attention as the modern scientist or mathematician. The rewards are in proportion.

The simplest way to get at Joyce's technique in language, as well as to see its relation to TV, is to consider the principle of the electronic tube. The paradox of the electronic tube is that it is the means of breaking the conductor in an electric circuit. The tube permits the electrons to escape from the wire that ordinarily conveys them. But the tube controls the conditions of escape. It liberates electrons from the wire but it provides a new context in which they can be repatterned. The cathode inside the tube is one end of the broken conductor and the anode is the other. The anode attracts and receives the billions of electrons that are "boiled" off the surface of the cathode. When a tube is connected into an alternating-current circuit, the anode is positive during half of each cycle. During the half cycle when the anode is negative, electrons cannot reach the anode. It is this characteristic of an electronic tube which enables it to act as a rectifier, changing alternating currents into direct current.

The grid is the controlling or "valve" electrode of the tube. It is located between the cathode and the anode in the path of the electrons. By voltage control the grid acts as trigger for the electronic flow. Grid bias blocking electronic flow is recentralized by signal voltage. Signal voltage is a trigger that releases full flow of current through the tube. But this flow stops when anode voltage becomes negative. Cycle then repeats. The load of current on this cycle is a motor.

When current is too weak for direct flow, it can, in a vacuum tube, be used as signal voltage on the grid of the tube. Then every variation in the shape of the wave will be faithfully reproduced in the output wave of the tube. Thus a tiny amount of energy can be exactly controlled or stepped up instantly to very high potentials.

Now metaphor has always had the character of the cathode-anode circuit, and the human ear has always been a grid, mesh, or, as Joyce calls it in *Finnegans Wake*, Earwicker. But Joyce was the first artist to make these aspects of language and communication explicit. In so doing, he applied the principles of electronics to the whole history of culture. The entire cyclic body of *Finnegans Wake* is suspended between a predicate and a subject. The cathode-anode aspect of metaphor and language Joyce first extended to syntax. He took the charge of meaning out of the wire of direct statement into the vacuum-tube of the self-contained poetic drama of his "all nights newsery reel."

Metaphor means a carrying across. All speech is metaphoric because any oral sound is a gesture towards externalizing an inner gesture of the mind. The auditory situation is a gesture towards externalizing an inner gesture of the mind. The auditory situation is a carrying across from a silent situation. Writing is metaphor for sound. It translates, or metamorphizes the audible into the visual. There is necessarily discontinuity in metaphor. There has to be a leap from one situation to another. If I say: "I'll take a rain-check on that," I am breaking the wire of direct reply: "Sorry, can't make it," and creating an independent circuit. A social situation is carried across to a sporting event which is discontinuous with, but proportioned to it. The new circuit sets up a drama which reshapes and controls the initial situation. The social situation of refusal is transformed by the sporting situation of disappointment and deferred pleasure. A great deal of energy plays back and forth between these two poles. With a minimum of signal voltage, "rain-check" creates the mood of informality and spontaneous regret. All metaphors can, of course, be reduced to the four-part ratio as here: "My feelings in refusing your invitation—are to my usual feelings in such formalities—as when weather refuses to permit me—to see a ball game." Or, "my feelings about your social invitation are positive even when the feelings about the deferred game are negative."

Joyce carried these four-fold intellectual proportions into every gesture and situation in the *Wake*. That is why it is always radiant with intelligibility when seen or apprehended. Here Comes Everybody is his cathode, Anna Livia Plurabelle his anode, and Earwicker or Persse O'Reilly his grid or triggerman. We are the main circuit into which this electronic tube is connected. We can thus see that the functions of a work of art, or electronic tube in the social circuit, are manifold. Principally, however, the tube provides a means of control which can step up the feeble signal voltage to greater intensities of manifestation. The tube permits multiple re-shaping of the ordinary current of small talk and gossip for many kinds of work. It is no exaggeration to say that all things in this "funanimal" world were current for the tube of the *Wake*. All the social currents that ever were, Joyce can easily adopt in the vacuum tube, or head, or glass house of the sleeping giant Finnegan. "This is modeln times." The plasticity of human experience can now be modelled in any shape desired. The nature of electricity applied to existing information about past and present tends by virtue of its instantaneous character to abolish the past and to waken the sleeping giant Finnegan who is the collective experience of mankind. Joyce saw that communication in modern times had altered our relations to the past and to ourselves. At the Renaissance the mechanical aids to knowledge had created an image of interstellar space which swallowed man. Today, a new technology of great delicacy and precision has created an image of ourselves which invites us to swallow nature. The gap between man and the world, art and nature, has been abolished. Toward the end of the *Wake*, Here Comes Everybody says:

"Well, yeamen, I have bared my whole past, I flatter myself, on both sides . . . and, as a matter of fact, I undertake to discontinue all practices. . . ."

The guilt of HCE or everyman has been probed from so many angles and has raised so many issues that the glass house of his memories is now an open secret. At this point the four old men who have been quizzing him yield to another group:

"We bright young chaps of the brand new brain-trust are briefed here and with maternal sanction. . . . All halt! Sponsor program and close down. That's enough general, of finicking about Finnegan and fiddling with his gaddles. . . . His thoughts that would be words, his livings that have been deeds . . . and tell you people here who have had the phoney habit (it was remarketable) in his clairaudience . . . to bring ruptures to our roars now I am amp amp amplify. . . ." The young brain-trust, representative of twentieth-century science and broadcasting, brush aside the nightmare of the past, they summon the uttermost powers, and the whole newsery reel of the sons and daughters of Anna Livia Plurabelle fades into the new day.

NOTES ON BURROUGHS

1. Today men's nerves surround us; they have gone outside as electrical environment. The human nervous system itself can be reprogramed biologically as readily as any radio network can alter its fare. Burroughs has dedicated *Naked Lunch* to the first proposition, and *Nova Express* to the second. *Naked Lunch* records private strategies of culture in the electric age. *Nova Express* indicates some of the "corporate" responses and adventures of the Subliminal Kid who is living in a universe which seems to be someone else's insides. Both books are a kind of engineer's report of the terrain hazards and mandatory processes which exist in the new electric environment.

2. Burroughs uses what he calls "Brion Gysin's cut-up method which I call the fold-in method." To read the daily newspaper in its entirety is to encounter the method in all its purity. Similarly, an evening watching television programs is an experience in a corporate form—an endless succession of impressions and snatches of narrative. Burroughs is unique only in that he is attempting to reproduce in prose what we accommodate every day as a commonplace aspect of life in the electric age. If the corporate life is to be rendered on paper, the method of discontinuous non-story must be employed.

3. That man provides the sexual organs of the technological world seems obvious enough to Burroughs, and such is the stage (or "biological theatre" as he calls it in *Nova Express*) for the series of social orgasms brought about by the evolutionary mutations of man and society. The logic, physical and emotional, of a world in which we have made our environment out of our own nervous systems, Burroughs follows everywhere to the peripheral orgasm of the cosmos.

4. Each technological extension involves an act of collective cannibalism. The previous environment with all its private and social values, is swallowed by the new environment and reprocessed for whatever values are digestible. Thus, Nature was succeeded by the mechanical environment and became what we call the "content" of the new industrial environment. That is, Nature became a vessel of aesthetic and spiritual values. Again and again the old environment is upgraded into an art form while the new conditions are regarded as corrupt and degrading. Artists, being experts in sensory awareness, tend to concentrate on the environmental as the challenging and dangerous situation. That is why they may seem to be "ahead of their time." Actually, they alone have the resources and temerity to live in immediate contact with the environment of their age. More timid people prefer to accept the content, the previous environment's values, as the continuing reality of their time. Our natural bias is to accept the new gimmick (automation, say) as a thing that can be accommodated in the old ethical order.

5. During the process of digestion of the old environment, man finds it expedient to anesthetize himself as much as possible. He pays as little attention to the action of the environment as the patient heeds the surgeon's scalpel. The gulping or swallowing of Nature by the machine was attended by a complete change of the ground rules of both the sensory ratios of the individual nervous system and the patterns of the social order as well. Today, when the environment has become the extension of the entire mesh of the nervous system, anesthesia numbs our bodies into hydraulic jacks.

6. Burroughs disdains the hallucinatory drugs as providing mere "content," the fantasies, dreams that money can buy. Junk (heroin) is needed to turn the human body itself into an environment that includes the universe. The central theme of *Naked Lunch* is the strategy of by-passing the new electric environment by becoming an environment oneself. The moment one achieves this environmental state all things and people are submitted to you to be processed. Whether a man takes the road of junk or the road of art, the entire world must submit to his processing. The world becomes his "content." He programs the sensory order.

7. For artists and philosophers, when a technology is new it yields Utopias. Such is Plato's *Republic* in the 5th century B. C., when

phonetic writing was being established. Similarly. More's *Utopia* is written in the sixteenth century when the printed book had just become established. When electric technology was new and speculative, *Alice in Wonderland* came as a kind of non-Euclidean space-time Utopia, a grown-up version of which is the *Illuminations* of Rimbaud. Like Lewis Carroll, Rimbaud accepts each object as a world and the world as an object. He makes a complete break with the established procedure of putting things *into* time or space:

> That's she, the little girl behind the rose bushes, and she's dead. The young mother, also dead, is coming down the steps. The cousin's carriage crunches the sand. The small brother (he's in India!) over there in the field of pinks, in front of the sunset. The old men they've buried upright in the wall covered with gilly-flowers.

But when the full consequences of each new technology have been manifested in new psychic and social forms, then the anti-Utopias appear. *Naked Lunch* can be viewed as the anti-Utopia of *Illuminations*:

> During withdrawal the addict is acutely aware of his surroundings. Sense impressions are sharpened to the point of hallucination. Familiar objects seem to stir with a writhing furtive life. The addict is subject to a barrage of sensations external and visceral.

Or, to give a concrete example from the symbolist landscape of *Nova Express*:

> A guard in a uniform of human skin, black buck jacket with carious yellow teeth buttons, an elastic pullover skirt in burnished Indian copper . . . sandals from calloused foot soles of young Malayan farmer . . .

The key to symbolist perception is in yielding the permission to objects to resonate with their *own* time and space. Conventional pictorial and literary perception seeks to put diverse objects into the *same* time and space. Time and space themselves are subjected to the uniform and continuous visual processing that provides us with the "connected and rational" world that is in fact only an isolated fragment of reality—the visual. There is no uniform and continuous character in the non-visual modalities of space and time. The symbolists freed themselves from visual conditions into the visionary world of the iconic and the auditory. Their art, to the visually oriented and literary man, seems haunted, magical and often incomprehensible. It is, in John Ruskin's words,

*... the expression, in a moment, by a series of symbols thrown
together in bold and fearless connections, of truths which it would have
taken a long time to express in any verbal way, and of which the
connection is left for the beholder to work out for himself; the gaps, left
or overleaped by the haste of the imagination, forming the grotesque
character.* (Modern Painters)

The art of the interval, rather than the art of the connection, is not
only medieval but Oriental; above all, it is the art mode of instant
electric culture.

8. There are considerable antecedents for the Burroughs attempt
to read the language of the biological theatre and the motives of the
Subliminal Kid. *Fleurs du Mal* is a vision of the city as the technological extension of man. Baudelaire had once intended to title the book
Les Limbes. The vision of the city as a physiological and psychic
extension of the body he experienced as a nightmare of illness and
self-alienation. Wyndham Lewis, in his trilogy *The Human Age*,
began with *The Childermass*. Its theme is the massacre of innocents
and the rape of entire populations by the popular media of press and
film. Later in *The Human Age* Lewis explores the psychic mutations
of man living in "the magnetic city," the instant, electric and angelic
(or diabolic) culture. Lewis views the action in a much more inclusive
way than Burroughs whose world is a paradigm of a future in which
there can be no spectators but only participants. All men are totally
involved in the insides of all men. There is no privacy and no private
parts. In a world in which we are all ingesting and digesting one
another there can be no obscenity or pornography or decency. Such
is the law of electric media which stretch the nerves to form a global
membrane of enclosure.

9. The Burroughs diagnosis is that we can avoid the inevitable
"closure" that accompanies each new technology by regarding our
entire gadgetry as *junk*. Man has hopped himself up by a long series
of technological fixes:

*You are dogs on all tape. The entire planet is being developed into
terminal identity and complete surrender.*

We can forego the entire legacy of Cain (the inventor of gadgets) by
applying the same formula that works for *junk*—"apomorphine"
extended to all technology:

> *Apomorphine is no word and no image. . . . It is simply a question of putting through an innoculation program in the very limited time that remains—Word begets image and image is virus.*

Burroughs is arguing that the power of the image to beget image, and of technology to reproduce itself via human intervention, is utterly in excess of our power to control the psychic and social consequences:

> *Shut the whole thing right off. Silence—when you answer the machine you provide it with more recordings to be played back to your "enemies." Keep the whole nova machine running—the Chinese character for "enemy" means to be similar to or to answer—Don't answer the machine—Shut it off—*

Merely to be in the presence of any machine, or replica of our body or faculties, is to close with it. Our sensory ratios shift at once with each encounter with any fragmented extension of our being. This is a non-stop express of innovation that cannot be endured indefinitely:

> *We are just dust falls from demagnetized patterns—Show business.*

It is the medium that is the message because the medium creates an environment that is as indelible as it is lethal. To end the proliferation of lethal new environmental expression, Burroughs urges a huge collective act of restraint as well as a non-closure of sensory modes— "The biological theater of the body can bear a good deal of new program notes."

10. *Finnegans Wake* provides the closest literary precedent to Burroughs' work. From beginning to end it is occupied with the theme of "the extensions" of man—weaponry, clothing, languages, number, money and media *in toto*. Joyce works out in detail the sensory shifts involved in each extension of man, and concludes with the resounding boast:

> *The keys to. Given!*

Like Burroughs, Joyce was sure he had worked out the formula for total cultural understanding and control. The idea of art as total programing for the environment is tribal, mental, Egyptian. It is, also, an idea of art to which electric technology leads quite strongly. We live science fiction. The bomb is our environment. The bomb is of higher learning all compact, the extension division of the university.

The university has become a global environment. The university now contains the commercial world, as well as the military and government establishments. To reprogram the cultures of the globe becomes as natural an undertaking as curriculum revision in a university. Since new media are new environments that reprocess psyche and society in successive ways, why not bypass instruction in fragmented subjects meant for fragmented sections of the society and reprogram the environment itself? Such is Burroughs' vision.

11. It is amusing to read reviews of Burroughs that try to classify his books as non-books or as failed science fiction. It is a little like trying to criticize the sartorial and verbal manifestations of a man who is knocking on the door to explain that flames are leaping from the roof of our home. Burroughs is not asking merit marks as a writer; he is trying to point to the shut-on button of an active and lethal environmental process.

The End of the Work Ethic

AN ADDRESS BY
Prof. H. Marshall McLuhan, c.c., m.a., ph.d.
DIRECTOR, CENTRE FOR CULTURE AND TECHNOLOGY,
UNIVERSITY OF TORONTO

CHAIRMAN
The President, Joseph H. Potts
EMPIRE CLUB OF CANADA

Mr. Potts

There is a tendency in the human species, well recognized by psychologists, for those of lesser stature to emulate or at least to discover some common denominator, to share with a man or a woman of distinction.

I am not certain whether or not this is indicative of an inferiority complex but, in any event, I confess that I am no exception, particularly in respect to today's distinguished guest.

You may well ask—what in the name of goodness do I have in common with Dr. McLuhan?—my answer, in all humility, is that we are both squares—I hasten to add, however, that we are squares not in a derogatory sense.

Each of us earned, or if you prefer, we acquired, two Bachelor of Arts Degrees.

When these are listed after our names, they appear, in proper mathematical parlance, as (BA) to the second power or, in common parlance, as BA squared.

Needless to say, Dr. McLuhan leaves me in the dust at that point.

He is also an MA squared and a Doctor of Letters to the seventh power.

Sir, we are delighted to have you with us today. Indeed, we consider it a signal honour that you should do so, particularly in view of the heavy demands upon your time and talents.

When I wrote to our guest last May and extended to him an invitation to address the Club during the current season, I also forwarded to him a copy of our Year Book.

Shortly thereafter I received a very gracious letter in which he said:

> It is good of you to think of me for The Empire Club. I shall be very pleased to speak to your members at lunch in the coming season.
>
> Many thanks for the Year Book. It reminds me, however, to mention that I never use a written manuscript for talks. I am sure something can be worked out.

I advised him that this presented no problem since all addresses to the Club are tape recorded.

The ability to deliver an address or talk without recourse to a written text is almost a lost art but our guest is in good company in this regard, with Mr. Caouette, who spoke to us last week and with John Fisher, who addressed us earlier in the season when we paid homage to another distinguished Canadian, A. Y. Jackson.

As you are undoubtedly aware, the Group of Seven were by no means acclaimed with open arms when they originally banded together to form the first Union of Artists in Canada.

Mr. Jackson made a reference to this when he addressed the Club in 1925. He said:

> There are a great many people interested in Canadian art today—more than ever before. That interest is sometimes like that of the old lady who was hurrying rapidly out of one of our Group exhibitions, and when asked why she was in such a hurry she explained, "I hate these pictures, but I am afraid if I stay around here longer I am going to like them."

I don't really expect that any of you are planning to rush out of this meeting, or you wouldn't have come in the first place.

But I can't guarantee that you will like, in the sense of agreeing with, that which you are going to hear but I'm sure we will find it stimulating and enjoyable.

Our guest is a distinguished academician, author and lecturer. He received the Governor General's Award for critical prose, the Carl-Einstein-Preis, West Germany Critics Award, the British Institute of Public Relations Presidential Medal, the Golden Medal of the President of the Republic of Italy and was appointed to the Schweitzer Chair at Fordham University.

In 1963, he was appointed by the President of the University of Toronto to create a new Centre for Culture and Technology (to study the psychic and social consequences of technologies and media). He was appointed as a Companion of the Order of Canada in 1970.

He is the author or co-author of some thirteen major works, including—

> *The Mechanical Bride: Folklore of Industrial Man*
> *The Gutenberg Galaxy: The Making of Typographic Man*
> *The Medium is the Massage*
> *Culture Is Our Business* and
> *Take Today: The Executive as Dropout*
>   which was published this year.

One of the finest tributes paid to our guest was by one of his contemporaries in reviewing *The Gutenberg Galaxy*:

> If McLuhan's way out it is because that's where we really are. His book opens directly and creatively out onto every humane activity known to man; it forces consideration of pressing up-to-date (futuristic, yet) problems in politics, economics, philosophy, literature, and post-Newtonian physics so as to leave many current jargons distantly relevant at best. It offers casual erudition that's appalling in scope and variety; it's shot with illuminations of men like Shakespeare, Pope, Swift, Blake, Ruskin, Rimbaud, and Joyce. It leaves an average professor of English like myself feeling somewhat of a cross between a dodo and an astronaut with a heart condition.

Ladies and gentlemen, it is my great pleasure to ask Professor McLuhan to speak to us on the subject: "The End of the Work Ethic."

Prof. H. Marshall McLuhan

It's not that seagulls are stupid, they are very wild and very emotional. They just can't be trained like eagles, hawks and ravens.

I have a friend on the Faculty, Professor John Abrams who went to Russia a few months ago. Before he started out, I asked him: "John, please pick up a couple of authentic Russian stories for me. I'd like to know just what sort of stories they tell in Russia." In due time, he relayed a couple to me:

One story concerned a yokel visitor to Moscow, who was a bit of a provincial, was oohing and ahing over "this wonderful city" and thanking God for "our wonderful subways" and "our wonderful economy" and "our wonderful stores" and "our wonderful people." His acquaintance remonstrated: "You don't thank God, you thank Stalin." And the visitor said: "Sure, but what if Stalin dies? Then you *really* can thank God."

The other story concerns a Russian attempt to set up an American-style nightclub:

The nightclub failed and they had a little investigation. The committee inquired: "Well, what did you do? How about the decor? What was the setting?" "Well", they said, "we had top Italian designers, with Hollywood advice and suggestions." "And how about the food?" They said: "It was splendid. We had French chefs, nothing but the best wines, modest prices, and everybody seemed pleased." "And how about the girls?" "Well, they were super, too. Every one of them had been a Party member since 1918."

There's an undercurrent of grievance in all good jokes, as you may have noticed. Take the story about a man who went to Kennedy Airport not long ago, to pick up an Irish friend for whom it was the first visit to the U.S.A.:

As they drove into New York, the Irishman was fascinated by the advertisements. When he saw an ad: *USE EX-LAX—BE YOUNGER,* he said: "What is it?" Said the friend: "There's a drug store right here. I'll stop and get you some." And he bought a cake of *Ex-Lax* which the Irishman proceeded to consume. After a while, the friend said: "Are you feeling any younger?" And the Irishman showed a certain amount of hesitation, but he said: "I'm not sure—but I've just done something very childish!"

Jokes are mostly concerned with grievances, and when new kinds of jokes appear, you can depend upon it, there is some sort of uncomfortable abrasive area of tension developing in the community. The Newfie jokes represent a certain amount of mild irritation relating to group maladjustment. Most of us have heard some of the "good news/bad news" jokes that project a sort of gripe about the rise of the new subjective journalism and the disappearance of the old objective journalism. I'll have a chance, perhaps, to refer to examples later. The old journalism had attempted to be "objective" and detached. For many years this meant giving "both sides" at once—the pro and the con—the yes and the no—the for and against—the black and the white. When you give both "sides" at once, you are in the tradition of "objective" reporting. If something is about to be done in the community, you explain what's against it and what's for it. On the other hand, the new journalism is an attempt to give "all sides at once" by simply immersing you in the total situation, Norman Mailer style, or Truman Capote style (*In Cold Blood*). Norman Mailer's *Miami and the Siege of Chicago* is not so much a report about the convention or the candidates or the policies of the parties. Rather, Mailer plunges us into a "happening" for the feel of it. The new journalism is subjective immersion. Whether it's fact or fiction, doesn't matter any more. When you get all sides at once, it is a sort of fiction anyway. So, Norman Mailer's subtitle on his *Armies of the Night* is: "History as novel—novel as history," pointing to the loss of boundaries between reporting and fiction. When we say: "He made the news," we point to the fact of news as fiction, as something *made*. Perhaps that is why there is always just enough news every day to fill every paper, with nothing left over.

Now, I am going to turn to my topic at once, so I will not be accused of not having gotten around to it. "The End of the Work Ethic" is quite directly related to the fact that under electric conditions of the new information environment it is no longer possible to have a mere goal. When everything happens at once, when you are inundated with information from every quarter of the globe at once, and every day, you cannot fix a distant objective and say: "I'm going to move toward that point." That point is already in rapid motion, as you are, and long before you take a step in that direction, everything will have changed.

The work ethic, insofar as it meant private goal orientation, is not practical and disappeared some time ago. But, related to this situation is change in the *job*. The job will no longer hold up—it's too specialized an action for the electric age. The job as specialism, as a fixed position in an organization chart, will not hold up against the simultaneous jostling and the interfacing of simultaneous information. What is taking the place of the job is *role-playing*. When you are moonlighting and starlighting, that is role-playing; and most people are doing this in some degree or other. The job-holder drops out as the consultant drops in.

Role-playing, in effect, means having more than one job. A housewife is a role-player because she has many jobs, and so do farm-

ers and many other people in the community. They are not essentially job-holders, but role-players. Notice the stress on "playing." I
am going to bear down on that theme a bit. Electrically, we are moving into an age of play which will bring many new patterns of work
and learning. There is about to appear from a Canadian publisher a
book called *The Leisure Riots*. It concerns a rebellion of a community
against a group of executives who are trying to transform fun and
games, and leisure-time activities, into industrial packages. When
skiing or hockey or football or tourism become encumbered with
equipment and consumer packages and are made expensive and difficult, they cease to be fun. The *play* has gone. This is a situation which
is reflected in various aspects of our world at present. It is another
area of grievance. The idea of play and recreation has gained much
new meaning in this age, not only from such classic studies as *Homo
Ludens* by J. Huizinga, but from quantum mechanics. Huizinga
relates the *play* principle to the development of all our institutions, so
that the very idea of "party government" implies the interplay of
diverse attitudes and policies as a means of equilibrium and social
adaptation. In chemistry and new compounds, the very fact of the
chemical bond has become the *resonant interval* of interfacing particles. Matter is now seen to be constituted by resonating intensities of
interplay, minus any *connections* whatever.

All are familiar with the *play* between the wheel and the axle as the
very principle of mobility, and we seek to avoid the up-tight, on one
hand, or the too slack, on the other hand. But it could be argued that
the dropout is a victim of the up-tight situation and that he drops out
in order to regain "touch." When the wheel and the axle get too close,
they too, lose touch. When they are too distant, they collapse. To be
"in a bind" is to lose touch as much as when we become too remote.
When a group of viable people volunteered to enter mental institutions as if they were in need of therapy, the staff was unable to detect
their sanity, but the seriously deranged pointed at the intruders at
once, saying: "They're *playing*." Without play, there looms the
shadow of madness in private as in corporate life, whence the danger
of specialism and bureaucracy when the rigors of classification overlay
the relaxed countenance of harmonious faculties. The artist is always
at leisure because he must keep his mind at play, and he is never more
at leisure than when seeking the solution of tough technical problems.

Let me refer to an item from *Business Week* of last month—"The Case Against Executive Mobility." The theme is quite simple, and relates to the recognition that frequent transfers to new homes and places of work have become a sterile way of life in North America. To pull up stakes and move families as a means of advancing up the corporate ladder is no longer considered a very practical or reward-ing thing by big business. Another observation, in the same way, belittles a chance for significant job promotion that would affect the emotional lives of school-age children. At the other extremes, local I.B.M. operations have become so large that executives can often get the effects of diversified managerial experience they need for advancement without moving anywhere. To move people around quickly is to cease to have a community.

The current best-seller, *Jonathan Livingston Seagull*, is a kind of side-swipe or spoof on the Protestant work ethic. If the words "Jonathan Livingston" suggest the great medical missionary of the last century, the word "Seagull" is rich in aerial and spiritual suggestion. In fact, J. L. S. is a very hard-working and very aspiring individual whose endeavours are richly rewarded by rapid advancement aided by delightful skyscapes and photographs. We read how J. L. S. never ceases from practising all manner of flight techniques: "A hundred feet in the sky, he lowered his webbed feet, lifted his beak and strained to hold the painful, hard-twisting curves of his wings." Of course, the idea of elevation and levitation are easily associated with the strenuous and precise manoeuvers of the seagull. However, he soon phases him-self out of all polarity in the company by the sheer speed of his success.

Since a seagull never speaks back to the council flock, Jonathan's voice was raised in exhortation: "Irresponsibility, my brothers? Who is more responsible than a gull who finds and follows a meaning, a higher purpose for life? For a thousand years we have scrabbled after fish heads but now we have a reason to live, to learn, to discover, to be free. Give me one chance, let me show you what I've found. The flock might as well have been stone." But that didn't stop them from moving up the organization tree very fast into another dimension altogether, where he encountered a voice: "How do you expect us to fly as you fly? You are special and gifted and divine above other birds." Look at Fletcher, Lowell, Charles Rowland, Judy Lee—are they also special, gifted, divine? No more than you are. No more than I am. The only difference, the very only one, is that they began to understand what they really were, and they began to practise it.

Now the toil for self advancement and self perfection is one that belongs to the work ethic, allegorically spoofed in this book. Perhaps the success of the book has been that the reader can take it both ways at once, either as a critique or a panegyric of the old work ethic.

To return to the theme of the obsolescing of the work ethic in a world of electric information, it is helpful to understand that the public today has taken on a new role. Because of the very simultaneity of electric information and programming, there really are no more spectators; everybody has become a member of the cast. The consumer function itself, as it were, is outmoded. On Spaceship Earth there are no passengers, but all are crew.

Just how quickly the public participation flips from audience to actor has recently been noticed in Watergate, and earlier in the trial of Lieutenant Calley. When audience participation becomes too extensive, the villains on trial flip into public heroes because the audience quickly identifies with them, especially when they are men who are carrying out robot-like activities which necessarily resemble those of the average audience. When the audience identifies with a villain on trial, the public at first begins to feel villainous and guilty itself, and then resolves the problem by flipping the villain into the role of a "culture hero." Another situation in which the opportunities for public participation are very dramatic has been discovered by the hijackers of aeroplanes and other public services. One of the principal causes or motives for hijacking was precisely the desire for coverage and public attention on the part of these unhappy performers. So attractive is this form of notoriety and coverage, that the reporting of these events has had to cease. Perhaps we can get into the situation of today via the remark of the little boy on his first aeroplane ride. Once they had taken off, he said: "Daddy, when do we start to get smaller?" The little boy's question is rather complex since it is plain that the plane gets smaller, while the cabin does not. The little boy would never have asked such a question in an open cockpit plane, for not only does the plane get smaller, but the occupants also feel increasingly insignificant. However, the enclosed space of the cabin of the plane presents a very special kind of structure, namely, a visual space; that is, a space or *figure* without a *ground*.

Visual space has peculiar properties that are not shared by spaces created by any of the other senses. Visual space is continuous, uniform, connected and static, whereas the sense of touch, like the sense of hearing or smell, is discontinuous, disconnected, non-uniform and dynamic. Such is also the case with acoustic space, the space in which we all live in the electric age. To a considerable degree, Western literate man in the nineteenth century lived in visual space which he thought of as normal, natural, rational space. With the advent of a world environment of simultaneous and instantaneous information, Western man shifted from visual to acoustic space, for acoustic space is a sphere whose centre is everywhere and whose boundaries are nowhere. Such is the space created by electric information which arrives simultaneously from all quarters of the globe. It is a space which phases us out of the world of logical continuity and connected stability into the space-time world of the new physics in which the mechanical bond is the resonant interval of *touch* where there are no connections, but only interfaces.

Many people may still suppose that these matters belong to the realm of speculation and obstruse scientific investigation, but the present fact is that we all live in this new resonating, simultaneous world in which the relation between *figure* and *ground*, public and performer, goal-seeking and role-playing, centralism and decentralism, have simply flipped and reversed again and again. Civilized man, Euclidean man, whose visual faculties were sharpened and specialized by Graeco-Roman literacy, this kind of aggressive, goal-seeking, one-way entrepreneur, has simply been dislodged and put out of countenance by the new man-made environment of simultaneous electric information. It is important for survival to understand that the simultaneous data of the omnipresent information environment is itself *structurally* acoustic. When people understand this acoustic structure as their new habitat, they will at once recognize the risks for the strange goings-on in the human psyche and in human society in the effort to relate to this new habitat. It goes without saying that any of our senses adjusts at once to any change in levels of light or heat or sound, and so it is with the changes in the environmental structure that is constituted by the information services of our twentieth-century world. Instantaneous retrieval systems and data processing alter entirely the nature of decision-making. The old job-holder, secure in his niche in the organization chart, finds himself an Ishmael wandering about in a chaos of unrelated data.

Let me try to make this matter more vividly comprehensible by relating a story which concerned my own first discovery of acoustic space. A group of us which included Carl Williams (now President of the University of Western Ontario), Tom Easterbrook (Political Economy, University of Toronto), and Jacqueline Tyrwhitt (Architecture and Town Planning) were discussing the newest book of Siegfried Giedion, *The Beginnings of Architecture*. Jacqueline Tyrwhitt (she had worked with Giedion on this study for years) was explaining how Giedion presented the fact that the Romans were the first people to enclose space. The Egyptian pyramids enclosed no space since their interior was dark, as were their temples. The Greeks never enclosed any space, since they merely turned the Egyptian temples inside out, and a stone slab sitting on two columns is not an enclosed space. But the Romans, by putting the arch inside a rectangle, were the first to enclose space. (An arch itself is not an enclosed space since it is merely formed by tensile pressure and thrust.) However, when this arch is put inside a rectangle, as in the sections of a Roman viaduct or in the Arc de Triomphe, you have a genuine enclosed space, namely a visual space. Visual space is a static enclosure, arranged by vertical planes diagonally related. Thus, a cave is not an enclosed space any more than is a wigwam or a dome (Buckminster Fuller's domes manifest the acoustic principle rather than the visual or enclosed space principle). The wigwam, like the triangle, is not an enclosed space and is merely the most economical means of anchoring a vertical plane or object.

At this point, Carl Williams, the psychologist, objected that, after all, the spaces inside a pyramid, even though dark, could be considered as acoustic spaces, and he then mentioned the characteristic modes of acoustic space as a sphere whose centre is everywhere and whose margins are nowhere (which is, incidentally, the neo-Platonic definition of God). I have never ceased to meditate on the relevance of this acoustic space to an understanding of the simultaneous electric world. The basic structural fact about simultaneity is that the *effects* come before the *causes* in such structures, or, the *ground* comes before the *figure*. When the *figure* arrives, we say "the time is ripe."

Living electronically, where the effects come before the causes, is a rather graphic and vivid way of explaining why distant goals and objectives are somewhat meaningless to "neuronic" man. Electronic man, that is, works in a world whose electric services are an expansion into environmental form, of his own nervous system. To such a man is it meaningless to say that he should seek or pursue distant goals and objectives, since all satisfactions and objectives are already present to him. This explains the mystery of why preliterate and acoustic peoples appear to us to be so deeply satisfied with such shallow resources and means of existence. Acoustic man, living in a simultaneous environment of electric information, is suddenly disillusioned about the ideal of moreness, whether it be more goods or more people or more security or more fame. Acoustic, or electronic man, understands instantly that the nature and limits of human satisfactions forbid any increase of happiness through an increase of power or wealth. Acoustic man naturally "plays it by ear" and lives harmoniously and musically and melodiously. Ecology is only another name for this acoustic simultaneity and the sudden responsibility for creating ecological environments pressed very suddenly upon Western man on October 17th, 1959. That was the day when Sputnik went into orbit, putting this planet inside a man-made environment for the first time. As soon as the planet went inside a man-made environment, the occupants of the planet began to hum and sing the ecological theme song without any further prompting.

When the planet was suddenly enveloped by a man-made artifact, "Nature" flipped into art form. The moment of Sputnik was the moment of creating Spaceship Earth and/or the global theatre. Shakespeare at the Globe had seen all the world as a stage, but with Sputnik, the world literally became a global theatre with no more audiences, only actors.

Another theme with which we are acquainted today is that of the dropout, whether it be Agnew Agonistes or the school kid who cannot see how he can relate to the curriculum fare. It is also a theme in *Take Today: The Executive as Dropout* (Longman Canada, and Harcourt Brace Jovanovich, 1972—Marshall McLuhan and Barrington Nevitt) that the dropout is literally trying to "get in touch." This paradoxical fact is obscured to visual man, always looking for connections and unable to see any rationale in the dropout process. Earlier I had mentioned the example of the interval of play between the wheel and the axle as exemplifying the very nature of *touch*. To "keep in touch" is always to maintain a resonant interval of play between *figure* and *ground*, between our jobs and our lives, and between all of our interests and responsibilities. The paradoxical fact that touch is not connection but an interval, not a fixed position but a dynamic interface, helps to explain the changes from the work ethic of yesterday to the diversified role-playing demanded of us in the new electronic environment. Archie Bunker is extremely popular as exhibiting much of the discomfort that results from his being frequently subjected to new situations which are alien to his specialized emotional rigidities and his very particularized points of view that result from his having a *fixed position* at all times when looking at his world. Time was when a man's point of view was thought of as something integral and important. Today, to have a fixed position from which to examine the world, merely guarantees that one will not relate to a rapidly changing world. The problems in the Watergate hearings are notable exemplars of this new situation. Their expertise and highly specialized skills as advisers to the government bureaucracy seemed only to qualify them for involuntary show biz. They were a group of backroom confidants who were suddenly flushed out into the public eye as expendable.

Wyndham Lewis, the painter-writer, once said: "The artist is engaged in painting or describing the future in detail because he is the only person who knows how to live in the present." However, to live in the present, or to *take today now*, involves acceptance of the entire past as *now*, and the entire future as *present*. Science fiction doesn't really measure up to the everyday reality because the real has become fantastic. The future is not what it used to be, and it is now possible to predict the past in many scientific senses. With "carbon 14" tests available, we can now predict why we shall have to re-write most of the past, simply because we can see much more of it simultaneously. At electric speeds of information it is not only the assembly line that is outmoded by computer programming, but the organization chart that has been outmoded. On the one hand, we hear about new difficulties at the Ford and similar plants in getting workers to come full time. Two or three days a week seems to be as much as the Detroit worker feels necessary to be involved in gainful employment. Absenteeism means that most of the cars now turned out on Fridays and Mondays are duds. This results from having to staff the assembly lines at those periods of the week with substitutes who have perhaps never seen an assembly line before. The story is told in Arthur Hailey's *Wheels*.

The instantaneous, simultaneous programming which has succeeded the one-thing-at-a-time world of the assembly line is familiar to the IBM world. It is now possible to include all the assembly line programs of an entire enterprise on a few little "solid state" chips. Along with the flip from hardware sequence speeds, comes the flip from hardware scale to software programming. The shift from hardware quantity to software is nowhere more spectacular than in the micro-dot library contrived by Vannevar Bush for the use of the astronauts. He made it possible to include in the space the size of a pinhead, twenty million printed volumes in retrievable form.

One of the peculiarities of the reversals in this new world of the electric information environment, is the return of the mentality and the figure of the hunter, on a massive scale. Man-hunting, whether under the mode of commercial or military espionage, is one of the biggest businesses of the twentieth century. It is a world in which the vision of Edgar Allan Poe and the work of Sherlock Holmes merge to become a new kind of "work." It is a kind of aesthetic work of pattern recognition far removed from the Protestant work ethic of goal-seeking. Today the hunter, the engineer, the programmer, the researcher, and the aesthete are one.

Intimations of this coming change occurred as early as Carlyle's *Past and Present* (1843) in which he contrasted the world of his time with the life of a medieval monastery in which work and prayer combine to create community. As specialism and industrialism developed in the nineteenth century, the artists combined to confront and denounce the anti-humanism of this new mechanical world of fragmentation. Paradoxically, the aesthetes, from Ruskin and Pater to Oscar Wilde, agreed that art and work must blend once more to create good art and the good life. The medievalism of the pre-Raphaelites was not nostalgically motivated so much as concerned with the need of their time to recover an integral work and life pattern. Comically enough, medievalism has come upon us in the sixties and the seventies in the so-called "hippie" costume of international motley, which we associate with the dropouts. Shaggy hair and shattered jeans is worn by those who are "agin" the establishment, even as motley was the clown costume of the rebel against authority. International motley is not limited to any continent, nor did it originate in any theory or concept of dress. It is as spontaneous a thing as country music, or Bob Dylan's enunciation. The figures of Emperor and clown, of establishment and anti-establishment, represent an age-old conflict. Strangely, the clown is a kind of P.R. man for the Emperor, one who keeps the Emperor in touch with "where it's at," regaling him with jokes and gags which are frequently of a hostile intent.

The nineteenth-century revolution had been, in part, to substitute the laws of the market and the economy for the laws of Nature. Economists and sociologists sought to discover the Newtonian laws of the universe embedded in the market place. The Sputnik event was another thing altogether, which simply obsolesced the planet itself as Nature disappeared into an art form. Now, the moment of Sputnik was the moment of creating Spaceship Earth, and the Global Theatre which, as we have seen, transformed the spectators into actors. Today, therefore, everybody demands a positive participation in the world process. This, of course, is one of the marks of Women's Lib. Whereas the suffragettes had merely sought to gain the right to vote, women today sense that they are totally involved in the social process on a non-specialist basis, and want a large piece of the action. Watergate has shown how the top executives of any big operation are extremely vulnerable today, so the most confidential operations can be submitted to public scrutiny on a mass scale. The Watergate cast represented a very specialized group, so much so that not one of them was able to provide any examples of decision-making. However, they were able to dramatize the plight of the specialist at high levels who, in effect, has nothing to do with decisions. At electric speeds, nobody makes decisions, as it were, but everybody becomes participant in a complex situation for which he can take no responsibility whatever.

Another peculiar feature of this electric time is that people not only do not make decisions individually, but in terms of the movement of information, it is the *sender* who is *sent*. It is the user of the telephone who goes to Peking and back, and so it is with TV or radio.

When you are "on the air," you are everywhere at once. This is a power beyond that of the angels, according to Thomas Aquinas, for they can only be in one place at a time. This is one way of pointing to the revolution in the work ethic, since we haven't a clue as to how to adjust our traditional lives to this kind of instant transportation of whole populations. Moreover, it means that the information environment automatically involves everybody in the work of learning, for the user of a radio program, or a newspaper, or an advertisement, is assisting the community process as much as anybody in a classroom or on an assembly line. When you are watching a play or a ball game, you are working for the community. We live in a world of paradoxes because at electric speed all facets of situations are presented to us simultaneously. It used to be the specialty of "the Irish bull" to do this. For example, a recent example mentions an exchange between two chiropodists. One says: "I have taken the corns off half the crown heads of Europe." That particular one contains several contradictory facets and metaphors, but as a wag said: "A man's reach must exceed his grasp, or what's a metaphor?"

In the sixteenth century Gutenberg made every man a reader, creating vast new publics, and in our time Xerox has made every man a publisher, creating (via position papers) vast numbers of big committees. When Everyman becomes a publisher, the office boy can give the Pentagon papers to the world. Such papers are really position papers that may never have been read by anybody. On the other hand, from the point of view of the publishers, Xerox is a total invasion of copyright and all books go into the public domain via this new kind of access. One of the dominant effects of our electric time is the effect of speedup on decision-making and on awareness of innumerable patterns and processes which had been quite undetectable at slower speeds. In fact, electric speed is tantamount to X-ray in relation to all human activities, invading privacy in both the personal and in the political sectors alike, and creating new patterns of involvement and participation in all affairs.

What is called the "new journalism" is, in effect, "immersion" reporting in contrast to the old "objective" reporting. The old and new journalism, corresponding to the old nineteenth-century hardware and the new electric software and the old and new politics, match these accordingly. The old objective journalism had aimed at

giving "both sides" of the case, whereas the new "immersion" journalism simply plunges the reader into the experience of being on the
scene, or being part of the scene, in "you are there" style. Of course,
"you are there" is merely another name for movie and TV experience, but the old ideal of objectivity in reporting, of "giving both
sides at once," now appears in retrospect as an illusion. That is, to
give the "pro" and the "con" is worlds away from being objective,
since it is necessarily a point of view at a distance. In the days of
objective reporting, it was always taken for granted that the "news
behind the news," or the "inside story" was necessarily quite different
from the outside or objective view of the situation. The outside story
was "fit to print," and the inside story was "not fit to print," in the
style of conscious vs. subliminal investigation of human psychology.
It was Freud who began the "immersion" approach to the human
psyche and the reporting of the subliminal or inside story of human
motivations. Personally speaking, my own approach to media study
has always been to report the subliminal effects of our own technologies upon our psyches, to report not the program, but the impact of
the medium upon the human user. Surprisingly, this kind of reporting of the hidden *effects* of media creates much indignation. Many
people would rather die than defend themselves against these effects.
The corresponding flip from "objective" to "immersion" techniques
in politics presents itself in the form of a political shift from parties
and policies to images and services. That is, political parties and their
explicit policies have simply been obsolesced by the images presented
by the party leaders, on the one hand, and the services taken for
granted by the community, regardless of the party that happens to be
in power, on the other hand.

The drastic flip from "objective" to "immersion" reporting has
spawned a new genre of jokes which contrast to good news and bad
news in a style represented by such stories as that of the doctor who
reports to the patient: "I have some bad news for you. We cut off the
wrong leg. But there is some good news. The withered limb is beginning to show some signs of life!" Or the story of the master of the
group of galley slaves, who says: "Men, I have some good news for
you. You are going to have an extra noggin of rum today. But now
the bad news—the Captain wants to go water skiing!" And in even
briefer form—Othello says to Desdemona: "I have bad news for you.

I'm going to strangle you. Now I'll tell you the good news. I found your handkerchief!"

The "revolution" I have been describing in reporting and in politics is the theme of the book called *Deschooling* by Ivan Illich. The theme of the book is simply that since there is now more information outside the schools than inside, we should close the schools and let the young obtain their education in the general environment once more. What Illich fails to see is that when the answers are outside, the time has come to put the questions inside the school, rather than the answers. In other words, it is now possible to make the schools not a place for packaged information, but a place for dialogue and discovery. This new pattern is recorded in the observation that twentieth-century man is a person who runs down the street shouting: "I've got the answers. What are the questions?" There are various versions of this observation, some of them attributed to people like Gertrude Stein. At any rate, when information becomes totally environmental and instantaneous, it is impossible to have monopolies of knowledge or specialism, a fact which is extremely upsetting to nearly everybody in our present Establishments.

The loss of monopolies of knowledge and specialism is recorded in many fun books, like *Parkinson's Law* and *The Peter Principle* and *One-up-man-ship*. In fact, it is a basic principle that when new grievances occur, new jokes come with them. Another basic change resulting from electric speed, of course, is the shift from centralized to decentralized structures in every sector of community life. At the political level it is called "separatism," but it has been happening on a huge scale in business and in education, as well. In private life it is called "dropoutism." In fact, that is the theme of my book *Take Today: The Executive as Dropout*. The work ethic is being overlaid very quickly by these new forms of organization so that twentieth-century man not only experiences his subliminal life being pushed up into consciousness, but the daily process of living takes on an increasingly mythic or corporate participation in processes that had previously been kept down in the unconscious. It was Harold Innis in his essay on "Minerva's Owl" (prompted by his studies of the Canadian economy) who showed how the ordinary technologies of everyday life have effects upon us that are in no way dependent upon the uses for which their makers intended them. However, in the age of ecology, the age in which we recognize that everything affects everything, it is no longer possible to remain unaware of the effects of the things we make, on our psychic and social lives. We are living in a situation which has been called "future shock." Future shock, in fact, is "culture lag," that is, the failure to notice what is happening in the present.

Before you return to work, I will tell you the story about the artist, Rodin, who, as he was completing his work on his statue of "The Thinker," it being a very hot afternoon, turned to the sitter and said: "O.K. stupid—you can get down now!"

Thanks very much.

Professor McLuhan was thanked on behalf of The Empire Club by Mr. H. Ian Macdonald, a Past President of the Club.

Mr. MacDonald

Mr. President, if you will forgive me a personal observation but I couldn't help noticing after studying you and Marshall McLuhan in profile that in one sense I think you are becoming a more rounded square than the guest speaker today.

A few years ago the name of Marshall McLuhan became synonymous with the phrase, "The medium is the message." And about that time this country was engaged in one of its periodic states of self-flagellation with the face of doom appearing in every crystal ball. However, I recall one noted public figure suggesting that all we really needed was a "happy medium." No one has ever suggested that Marshall McLuhan is a medium but I am sure that after listening to his message today we have found him, indeed, a deep and perceptive social commentator.

Personally, in my own anachronistic way, I have never really thought of work as an ethical matter—rather I simply thought of it as a preferable state to slow starvation. However, the new world that you have sketched, Marshall, is infinitely to be preferred to either work or starvation and it is a privilege for me to express to you the appreciation which we all so clearly feel for your remarks today.

Thank you.

THE RELATION OF ENVIRONMENT TO ANTI-ENVIRONMENT

*U*nder the heading that "What exists is likely to be mis-allocated" Peter Drucker in *Managing for Results* discusses the structure of social situations. "Business enterprise is not a phenomenon of nature but one of society. In a social situation, however, events are not distributed according to the 'normal distribution' of a natural universe (that is, they are not distributed according to the bell-shaped Gaussian curve). In a social situation a very small number of events *at one extreme*—the first ten percent to twenty percent at most—account for ninety percent of all results; whereas the great majority of events accounts for ten percent or so of the results." What Drucker is presenting here is the environment as it presents itself for human attention and action. He is confronting the phenomenon of the imperceptibility of the environment as such. It is this factor that Edward T. Hall also tackles in *The Silent Language*. The ground rules, the pervasive structure, the overall pattern eludes perception except in so far as there is an anti-environment or a counter-situation constructed to provide a means of direct attention. Paradoxically, the ten percent of the typical situation that Drucker designates as the area of effective cause and as the area of opportunity, this small factor is the environment. The ninety percent area is the area of problems generated by the active power of the ten percent environment. For the environment is an active process pervading and impinging upon all the components of the situation. It is easy to illustrate this.

Any new technology, any extension or amplification of human faculties when given material embodiment, tends to create a new environment. This is as true of clothing as of speech, or script, or wheel. This process is more easily observed in our own time when several new environments have been created. To take only the latest one, TV, we find a handful of engineers and technicians in the ten percent area, as it were, creating a set of radical changes in the ninety percent area of daily life. The new TV environment is an electric circuit that takes as its content the earlier environment, the photograph and the movie in particular. It is in the interplay between the old and the new environments that there is generated an innumerable series of problems and confusions. They extend all the way from how to allocate the time of children and adults to the problem of pay-TV and TV in the classroom. The new medium of TV as an environment creates new occupations. As an environment, it is imperceptible except in terms of its content. That is, all that is seen or noticed is the old environment, the movie. But even the effects of TV on the movie go unnoticed, and the effects of the TV environment in altering the entire character of human sensibility and sensory ratios is completely ignored.

The content of any system or organization naturally consists of the preceding system or organization, and in that degree acts as a control on the new environment. It is useful to notice all of the arts and sciences as acting in the role of anti-environments that enable us to perceive the environment. In a business civilization we have long considered liberal study as providing necessary means of orientation and perception. When the arts and sciences themselves become environments under conditions of electric circuitry, conventional liberal studies whether in the arts or sciences will no longer serve as an anti-environment. When we live in a museum without walls, or have music as a structural part of our sensory environment, new strategies of attention and perception have to be created. When the highest scientific knowledge creates the environment of the atom bomb, new controls for the scientific environment have to be discovered, if only in the interest of survival.

The structural examples of the relation of environment to anti-environment need to be multiplied as a means of understanding the principles of perception and activity involved. The Balinese say: "We have no art—we do everything as well as possible." This is not an ironic but a merely factual remark. In a pre-literate society art serves as a means of merging the individual and the environment, not as a means of training perception upon the environment. Archaic or primitive art looks to us like a magical control built into the environment. Thus to put the artefacts from such a culture into a museum or anti-environment is an act of nullification rather than of revelation. Today what is called "Pop Art" is the use of some object in our own daily environment as if it were anti-environmental. Pop Art serves to remind us, however, that we have fashioned for ourselves a world of artefacts and images that are intended not to train perception or awareness but to insist that we merge with them as the primitive man merges with his environment. The world of modern advertising is a magical environment constructed to produce effects for the total economy but not designed to increase human awareness. We have designed schools as anti-environments to develop the perception and judgment of the printed word. There are no means of training provided to develop similar perception and judgment of any of the new environments created by electric circuitry. This is not accidental. From the development of phonetic script until the invention of the electric telegraph human technology had tended strongly towards the furtherance of detachment and objectivity, detribalization and individuality. Electric circuitry has quite the contrary effect. It involves in depth. It merges the individual and the mass environment. To create an anti-environment for such electric technology would seem to require a technological extension of consciousness itself. The awareness and opposition of the individual are in these circumstances as irrelevant as they are futile.

The structural features of environment and anti-environment appear in the age-old clash between professionalism and amateurism, whether in sport or in studies. Professional sport is environmental and amateur sport is anti-environmental. Professional sport fosters the merging of the individual in the mass and in the patterns of the total environment. Amateur sport seeks rather the development of critical awareness of the individual and most of all, critical awareness of the ground rules of the society as such. The same contrast exists for studies. The professional tends to specialize and to merge his being uncritically in the mass. The ground rules provided by the mass response of his colleagues serve as a pervasive environment of which he is uncritical and unaware.

The party system of government affords a familiar image of the relations of environment and anti-environment. The government as environment needs the opposition as anti-environment in order to be aware of itself. The role of the opposition would seem to be that of the arts and sciences in creating perception. As the government environment becomes more cohesively involved in a world of instant information, opposition would seem to become increasingly necessary but also intolerable. Opposition begins to assume the rancorous and hostile character of a Dew Line, or a Distant Early Warning System. It is important, however, to consider the role of the arts and sciences as Early Warning Systems in the social environment. The models of perception provided in the arts and sciences alike can serve as indispensable means of orientation to future problems well before they become troublesome.

The legend of Humpty-Dumpty would seem to suggest a parallel to the 10%–90% distribution of causes and effects. The impact that resulted in his fall brought into play a massive response from the social bureaucracy. But all the King's horses and all the King's men could not put Humpty-Dumpty back together again. They could not recreate the old environment, they could only create a new one. Our typical response to a disrupting new technology is to recreate the old environment instead of heeding the new opportunities of the new environment. Failure to notice the new opportunities is also failure to understand the new powers. This means that we fail to develop the necessary controls or anti-environments for the new environment. This failure leaves us in the role of automata merely.

W. T. Easterbrook has done extensive exploration of the relations of bureaucracy and enterprise, discovering that as soon as one becomes the environment, the other becomes an anti-environment. They seem to bicycle along through history alternating their roles with all the dash and vigor of tweedle-dum and tweedle-dee. In the eighteenth century when *realism* became a new method in literature, what happened was that the external environment was put in the place of anti-environment. The ordinary world was given the role of art object by Daniel Defoe and others. The environment began to be used as a perceptual probe. It became self-conscious. It became an "anxious object" instead of being an unperceived and pervasive pattern. Environment used as probe or art object is satirical because it draws attention to itself. The romantic poets extended this technique to external nature transforming nature into an art object. Beginning with Baudelaire and Rimbaud and continuing in Hopkins and Eliot and James Joyce, the poets turned their attention to language as a probe. Long used as an environment, language became an instrument of exploration and research. It became an anti-environment. It became Pop Art.

The artist as a maker of anti-environments permits us to perceive that much is newly environmental and therefore most active in transforming situations. This would seem to be why the artist has in many circles in the past century been called the enemy, the criminal. It helps to explain why news has a natural bias toward crime and bad news. It is this kind of news that enables us to perceive our world. The detective since Poe's Dupin has tended to be a probe, an artist of the big town, an artist-enemy, as it were. Conventionally, society is always one phase back, is never environmental. Paradoxically, it is the antecedent environment that is always being upgraded for our attention. The new environment always uses the old environment as its material.

In the Spring issue of the *Varsity Grad* (1965) Glenn Gould discusses the effects of recorded music on performance and composition. One of his main points is that as recorded music creates a new environment the audience in effect becomes participant both in performance and in composition. This is a reversal or chiasmus of form that occurs in any situation where an environment is pushed up into high intensity or high definition by technological change. A reversal of characteristics occurs as in the case with bureaucracy and enterprise. An environment is naturally of low intensity or low definition. That is why it escapes observation. Anything that raises the environment to high intensity, whether it be a storm in nature or violent change resulting from a new technology, such high intensity turns the environment into an object of attention. When an environment becomes an object of attention it assumes the character of an anti-environment or an art object. When the social environment is stirred up to exceptional intensity by technological change and becomes a focus of much attention, we apply the terms "war" and "revolution." All the components of "war" are present in any environment whatever. The recognition of war depends upon their being stepped up to high definition.

Under electric conditions of instant information movement both the concept and the reality of war become manifest in many of the situations of daily life. We have long been accustomed to war as that which goes on between publics or nations. Publics and nations were the creation of print technology. With electric circuitry the publics and nations became the content of the new technology: "The mass audience is not a public as environment but a public as content of a new electric environment." And whereas "the public" as an environment created by print technology consisted of separate individuals with varying points of view, the mass audience consists of the same individuals involved in depth in one another and involved in the creative process of the art or educational situation that is presented to them. Art and education were presented to the *public* as consumer packages for their instruction and edification. The new mass audience is involved immediately in art and education as participants and co-creators rather than as consumers. Art and education become new forms of experience, new environments, rather than new anti-environments. Pre-electric art and education were anti-environments in the sense that they were the content of various environments. Under electric conditions the content tends however towards becoming environmental itself. This was the paradox that Malraux found in *The Museum Without Walls*, and that Glenn Gould finds in recorded music. Music in the concert hall had been an anti-environment. The same music when recorded is *music without halls*, as it were.

Another paradoxical aspect of this change is that when music becomes environmental by electric means, it becomes more and more the concern of the private individual. By the same token and complementary to the same paradox the pre-electric music of the concert hall (the music when there was a public instead of a mass audience) was a corporate ritual for the group rather than the individual. This paradox extends to all electrical technology whatever. The same means which permit, for example, a universal and centralized thermostat do in effect encourage a private thermostat for individual manipulation. The age of the mass audience is thus far more individualistic than the preceding age of the *public*. It is this paradoxical dynamic that confuses every issue about "conformity" today and "separatism" and "integration." Profoundly contradictory actions and directions prevail in all of these situations. This is not surprising in an age of circuitry succeeding the age of the wheel. The feedback loop plays all sorts of tricks to confound the single plane and one-way direction of thought and action as they had been constituted in the pre-electric age of the machine.

Applying the above to the Negro question, one could say that the agrarian South has long tended to regard the Negro as environmental. As such, the Negro is a challenge, a threat, a burden. The very phrase "white supremacy" quite as much as the phrase "white trash" registers this environmental attitude. The environment is the enemy that must be subdued. To the rural man the conquest of Nature is an unceasing challenge. It is the Southerner who contributed the cowboy to the frontier. The Virginian, the archetypal cowboy as it were, confronts the environment as a hostile, natural force. To man on the frontier, other men are environmental and hostile. By contrast, to the townsmen, men appear not as environmental, but as content of the urban environment.

Parallel to the Negro question is the French Canada problem. The English Canadians have been the environment of French Canada since the railway and Confederation. However, since the telegraph and radio and television, French Canada and English Canada alike have become the content of this new technology. Electric technology is totally environmental for all human communities today. Hence the great confusion arising from the transformation of environments into anti-environments, as it were. All the earlier groupings that had constituted separate environments before electricity have now become anti-environments or the content of the new technology. As such, the old unconscious environments tend to become increasingly centres of acute awareness. The content of any new environment is just as unperceived as the old one had been initially. As a merely automatic sequence, the succession of environments and of the dramatics thereto appertaining, tend to be rather tiresome, if only because the audience is very prone to participate in the dramatics with an enthusiasm proportioned to its unawareness. In the electric age all former environments whatever become anti-environments. As such the old environments are transformed into areas of self-awareness and self-assertion, guaranteeing a very lively interplay of forces.

Eric Havelock in his book *Preface to Plato* has clarified the stages by which the written word served to detribalize the Greek world.

After the tribal encyclopedia of oral and memorized wisdom, writing enabled man to organize knowledge by categories and classifications; what Plato called the *ideas*. With the origin of classified data, or visual organization of knowledge, there came also representation in the arts. Representation is itself a form of matching or classifying, unknown to preliterate or native artists. Today we return to non-objective art, non-representational art, because in the electric age we are leaving the world of visual organization of experience.

The visual sense, alone of our senses, creates the forms of space and time that are uniform, continuous and connected. Euclidean space is the prerogative of visual and literate man. With the advent of electric circuitry and the instant movement of information, Euclidean space recedes and the non-Euclidean geometries emerge. Lewis Carroll, the Oxford mathematician, was perfectly aware of this change in our world when he took Alice through the looking glass into the world where each object creates its own space and conditions. To the visual or Euclidean man, objects do not create time and space. They are merely fitted into time and space. The idea of the world as an environment that is more or less fixed, is very much the product of literacy and visual assumptions. In his book *The Philosophical Impact of Modern Physics* Milic Capek explains some of the strange confusions in the scientific mind that result from the encounter of the old non-Euclidean spaces of preliterate man with the Euclidean and Newtonian spaces of literate man. The scientists of our time are just as confused as the philosophers, or the teachers, and it is for the reason that Whitehead assigned; they still have the illusion that the new developments are to be fitted into the old space or environment.

One of the most obvious areas of change in the arts of our time has not only been the dropping of representation, but the dropping of the story line. In poetry, in the novel, in the movie, narrative continuity has yielded to thematic variation. Such variation in place of story line or melodic line has always been the norm in native societies. It is now becoming the norm in our own society and for the same reason, namely that we are becoming a non-visual society.

In the age of circuitry, or feedback, fragmentation and specialism tend to yield to integral forms of organization. Humpty-Dumpty tends to go back together again. The bureaucratic efforts of all the

King's horses and all the King's men were naturally calculated to keep Humpty-Dumpty from ever getting together again. The Neolithic age, the age of the planter after the age of the hunter, was an age of specialism and division of labour. It has reached a somewhat startling terminus with the advent of electric circuitry. Circuitry is a profoundly decentralizing process. Paradoxically, it was the wheel and mechanical innovation that created centralism. The circuit reverses the characteristics of wheel, just as Xerography reverses the characteristics of the printing press. Before printing, the scribe, the author, and the reader tended to merge. With printing, author and publisher became highly specialized and centralized forms of action. With Xerography, author, and publisher, and reader tend to merge once more. Whereas the printed book had been the first mass-produced product, creating uniform prices and markets, Xerography tends to restore the custom-made book. Writing and publishing tend to become services of a corporate and inclusive kind. The printed word created the Public. The Public consists of separate individuals, each with his own point of view. Electric circuitry does not create a Public. It creates the Mass. The Mass does not consist of separate individuals, but of individuals profoundly involved in one another. This involvement is a function, not of numbers, but of speed. The daily newspaper is an interesting example of this fact. The items in the daily press are totally discontinuous and totally unconnected. The only unifying feature of the press is the date line. Through that date line the reader must go, as Alice went, "through the looking glass." If it is not today's date line, he cannot get in. Once he goes through the date line, he is involved in a world of items for which he, the reader, must write a story line. He makes the news, as the reader of a detective story makes the plot.

Just as the printed press created the Public as a new environment, so does each new technology or extension of our physical powers tend to create new environments. In the age of information, it is information itself that becomes environmental. The satellites and antennae projected from our planet, for example, have transformed the planet from being an environment into being a probe. This is a transformation which the artists of the past century have been explaining to us in their endless experimental models. Modern art, whether in painting, or poetry, or music, began as a probe and not as a package. The Symbolists literally broke up the old packages and put them into our hands as probes. And whereas the package belongs to a consumer age, the probe belongs to an age of experimenters.

One of the peculiarities of art is to serve as an anti-environment, a probe that makes the environment visible. It is a form of symbolic, or parabolic, action. Parable means literally "to throw against," just as symbol means "to throw together." As we equip the planet with satellites and antennae, we tend to create new environments of which the planet is itself the content. It is peculiar to environments that they are complex processes which transform their content into archetypal forms. As the planet becomes the content of a new information environment, it also tends to become a work of art. Where railway and machine created a new environment for agrarian man, the old agrarian world became an art form. Nature became a work of art. The Romantic movement was born. When the electric circuit went around the mechanical environment, the machine itself became a work of art. Abstract art was born.

As information becomes our environment, it becomes mandatory to program the environment itself as a work of art. The parallel to this appears in Jacques Ellul's *Propaganda* where he sees propaganda, not as an ideology or content of any medium, but as the operation of all the media at once. The mother tongue is propaganda because it exercises an effect on all the senses at once. It shapes our entire outlook and our ways of feeling. Like any other environment, its operation is imperceptible. When an environment is new, we perceive the old one for the first time. What we see on the late show is not TV, but old movies. When the Emperor appeared in his new clothes, his courtiers did not see his nudity, they saw his old clothes. Only the small child and the artist have that immediacy of approach that permits perception of the environmental. The artist provides us with anti-environments that enable us to see the environment. Such anti-environmental means of perception must constantly be renewed in order to be efficacious. That basic aspect of the human condition by which we are rendered incapable of perceiving the environment is one to which psychologists have not even referred. In an age of accelerated change, the need to perceive the environment becomes urgent. Acceleration also makes such perception of the environment more possible. Was it not Bertrand Russell who said that if the bath water got only half a degree warmer every hour, we would never know when to scream? New environments reset our sensory thresholds. These in turn, alter our outlook and expectations.

The need of our time is for the means of measuring sensory thresholds and of discovering exactly what changes occur in these thresholds as a result of the advent of any particular technology. With such knowledge in hand it would be possible to program a reasonable and orderly future for any human community. Such knowledge would be the equivalent of a thermostatic control for room temperatures. It would seem only reasonable to extend such controls to all the sensory thresholds of our being. We have no reason to be grateful to those who juggle the thresholds in the name of haphazard innovation.

THE AGENBITE
OF OUTWIT

ith the telegraph Western man began a process of putting his nerves outside his body. Previous technologies had been extensions of physical organs: the wheel is a putting outside ourselves of the feet, the city wall is a collective *outering* of the skin. But electronic media are, instead, extensions of the central nervous system, an inclusive and simultaneous field. Since the telegraph we have extended the brains and nerves of man around the globe. As a result, the electronic age endures a total uneasiness, as of a man wearing his skull inside and his brain outside. We have become peculiarly vulnerable. The year of the establishment of the commercial telegraph in America, 1844, was also the year Kirkegaard published *The Concept of Dread.*

A special property of all social extensions of the body is that they return to plague the inventors in a kind of *agenbite of outwit.* As Narcissus fell in love with an *outering* (projection, extension) of himself, man seems invariably to fall in love with the newest gadget or gimmick that is merely an extension of his own body. Driving an automobile or watching television, we tend to forget that what we have to do with is simply a part of ourselves stuck *out there.* Thus disposed, we become servo-mechanisms of our contrivances, responding to them in the immediate, mechanical way that they demand of us. The point of the Narcissus myth is not that people are prone to fall in love with their own images but that people fall in love with extensions of themselves which they are convinced are not extensions of themselves. This provides, I think, a fairly good image of all our technologies, and it directs us toward a basic issue, the idolatry of technology as involving a psychic numbness.

Every generation poised on the edge of massive change seems, to later observers, to have been oblivious of the issues and the imminent event. But it is necessary to understand the power of technologies to isolate the senses and thus, to hypnotize society. The formula for hypnosis is "one sense at a time." Our *private* senses are not closed systems but are endlessly translated into each other in the experience which we call consciousness. Our *extended* senses, tools or technologies, have been closed systems incapable of interplay. Every new technology diminishes sense interplay and awareness for precisely the area ministered to by that technology: a kind of identification of viewer and object occurs. This conforming of the beholder to the new form or structure renders those most deeply immersed in a revolution the least aware of its dynamic. At such times it is felt that the future will be a larger or greatly improved version of the *immediate past*.

The new electronic technology, however, is not a closed system. As an extension of the central nervous system, it deals precisely in awareness, interplay and dialogue. In the electronic age, the very instantaneous nature of the co-existence among our technological instruments has created a crisis quite new in human history. Our extended faculties and senses now constitute a single field of experience which demands that they become collectively conscious, like the central nervous system itself. Fragmentation and specialization, features of mechanism, are absent.

To the extent that we are unaware of the nature of the new electronic forms, we are manipulated by them. Let me offer, as an example of the way in which a new technology can transform institutions and modes of procedure, a bit of testimony by Albert Speer, German armaments minister in 1942, at the Nuremberg trials:

> The telephone, the teleprinter and the wireless made it possible for orders from the highest levels to be given direct to the lowest levels, where, on account of the absolute authority behind them, they were carried out uncritically; or brought it about that numerous offices and command centers were directly connected with the supreme leadership from which they received their sinister orders without any intermediary; or resulted in a widespread surveillance of the citizen; or in a high degree of secrecy surrounding criminal happenings. To the outside observer this governmental apparatus may have resembled the apparently chaotic confusion of lines at a telephone exchange, but like

the latter it could be controlled and operated from one central source. Former dictatorships needed collaborators of high quality even in the lower levels of leadership, men who could think and act independently. In the era of modern technique an authoritarian system can do without this. The means of communication alone permit it to mechanize the work of subordinate leadership. As a consequence a new type develops: the uncritical recipient of orders. (Quoted in Hjalmar Schacht, *Account Settled*, London, 1949.)

Television and radio are immense extensions of ourselves which enable us to participate in one another's lives, much as a language does. But the modes of participation are already built into the technology; these new languages have their own grammars.

The ways of thinking implanted by electronic culture are very different from those fostered by print culture. Since the Renaissance most methods and procedures have strongly tended toward stress on the *visual* organization and application of knowledge. The assumptions latent in typographic segmentation manifest themselves in the fragmenting of crafts and the specializing of social tasks. Literacy stresses *lineality*, a one-thing-at-a-time awareness and mode of procedure. From it derive the assembly line and the order of battle, the managerial hierarchy and the departmentalizations of scholarly decorum. Gutenberg gave us analysis and explosion. By fragmenting the field of perception and breaking information into static bits, we have accomplished wonders.

But electronic media proceed differently. Television, radio and the newspaper (at the point where it was linked with the telegraph) deal in *auditory space*, by which I mean that sphere of simultaneous relations created by the act of hearing. We hear from all directions at once; this creates a unique unvisualizable space. The all-at-once-ness of auditory space is the exact opposite of lineality, of taking one thing at a time. It is very confusing to learn that the mosaic of a newspaper page is "auditory" in basic structure. This, however, is only to say that any pattern in which the components co-exist without direct lineal hook-up or connection, creating a field of simultaneous relations, is auditory, even though some of its aspects can be seen. The items of news and advertising that exist under a newspaper dateline are interrelated only by that dateline. They have no interconnection of logic or statement. Yet they form a mosaic or corporate image whose parts are interpenetrating. Such is also the kind of order that tends to exist in a city or a culture. It is a kind of orchestral, resonating unity, not the unity of logical discourse.

The tribalizing power of the new electronic media, the way in which they return us to the unified fields of the old oral cultures, to tribal cohesion and pre-individualist patterns of thought, is little understood. Tribalism is the sense of the deep bond of family, the closed society as the norm of community. Literacy, the visual technology, dissolved the tribal magic by means of its stress on fragmentation and specialization, and created the individual. The electronic media, however, are group forms. Post-literate man's electronic media contract the world to a tribe or village where everything happens to everyone at the same time: everyone knows about, and therefore participates in, everything that is happening the moment it happens. Because we do not understand these things, because of the numbing power of the technology itself, we are helpless while undergoing a revolution in our North American sense-lives, via the television image. It is a charge comparable to that experienced by Europeans in the twenties and thirties, when the new radio "image" reconstituted overnight the tribal character long absent from European life. Our extremely visual world had immunity from the radio image, but not from the scanning finger of the TV mosaic.

It would be hard to imagine a state of confusion greater than our own. Literacy gave us an eye for an ear and succeeded in detribalizing that portion of mankind that we refer to as the Western world. We are now engaged in an accelerated program of detribalization of all backward parts of the world by introducing there our own ancient print technology at the same time that we are engaged in retribalizing ourselves by means of the new electronic technology. It is like becoming conscious of the unconscious, and of consciously promoting unconscious values by an ever clearer consciousness.

When we put our central nervous system outside us we returned to the primal nomadic state. We have become like the most primitive paleolithic man, once more global wanderers, but information gatherers rather than food gatherers. From now on the source of food, wealth and life itself will be information. The transforming of this information into products is now a problem for the automation experts, no longer a matter for the utmost division of human labor and skill. Automation, as we all know, dispenses with personnel. This terrifies mechanical man because he does not know what to do about the transition, but it simply means that work is finished, over and done with. The concept of work is closely allied to that of specialization, of special functions and non-involvement; before specialization there was no work. Man in the future will not work—automation will work for him—but he may be totally involved as a painter is, or as a thinker is, or as a poet is. Man works when he is partially involved. When he is totally involved he is at play or at leisure.

Man in the electronic age has no possible environment except the globe and no possible occupation except information-gathering. By simply moving information and brushing information against information, any medium whatever creates vast wealth. The richest corporation in the world, American Telephone and Telegraph, has only one function: moving information about. Simply by talking to one another, we create wealth. Any child watching a television program should be paid because he is creating wealth for the community. But this wealth is not money. Money is obsolete because it stores work (and work, as we have seen, is itself obsolete). In a workless, non-specialist society money is useless. What you need is a credit card, which is information.

When new technologies impose themselves on societies long habituated to older technologies, anxieties of all kinds result. Our electronic world now calls for a unified global field of awareness; the kind of private consciousness appropriate to literate man can be viewed as an unbearable kink in the collective consciousness demanded by electronic information movement. In this impasse, suspension of all automatic reflexes would seem in order. I believe that artists, in all media, respond soonest to the challenge of new pressures. I would like to suggest that they also show us ways of living with new technology without destroying earlier forms and achievements. The new media, too, are not toys; they should not be in the hands of Mother Goose and Peter Pan executives. They can be entrusted only to new artists.

Culture Without Literacy

*T*he ordinary desire of everybody to have everybody else think alike with himself has some explosive implications today. The perfection of the *means* of communication has given this average power-complex of the human being an enormous extension of expression.

"The telephone, the teleprinter and the wireless made it possible for orders from the highest levels to be given direct to the lowest levels, where, on account of the absolute authority behind them, they were carried out uncritically; or brought it about that numerous offices and command centres were directly connected with the supreme leadership from which they received their sinister orders without any intermediary; or resulted in a widespread surveillance of the citizen, or in a high degree of secrecy surrounding criminal happenings. To the outside observer this governmental apparatus may have resembled the apparently chaotic confusion of lines at a telephone exchange, but like the latter it could be controlled and operated from one central source. Former dictatorships needed collaborators of high quality even in the lower levels of leadership, men who could think and act independently. In the era of modern technique an authoritarian system can do without this. The means of communication alone permit it to mechanize the work of subordinate leadership. As a consequence a new type develops: the uncritical recipient of orders."[1]

Perfection of the *means* of communication has meant instantaneity. Such an instantaneous network of communication is the body-mind unity of each of us. When a city or a society achieves a diversity and equilibrium of awareness analogous to the body-mind network, it has what we tend to regard as a high culture.

But the instantaneity of communication makes free speech and thought difficult if not impossible and for many reasons. Radio extends the range of the casual speaking voice, but it forbids that many should speak. And when what is said has such range of control it is forbidden to speak any but the most acceptable words and notions. Power and control are in all cases paid for by loss of freedom and flexibility.

Today the entire globe has a unity in point of mutual inter-awareness which exceeds in rapidity the former flow of information in a small city—say Elizabethan London with its eighty or ninety thousand inhabitants. What happens to existing societies when they are brought into such intimate contact by press, picture stories, newsreels and jet propulsion? What happens when the neolithic Eskimo is compelled to share the time and space arrangements of technological man? What happens in our minds as we become familiar with the diversity of human cultures which have come into existence under innumerable circumstances, historical and geographical? Is not what happens comparable to that social revolution which we call the American melting-pot?

When the telegraph made possible a daily cross-section of the globe transferred to the page of newsprint, we already had our mental melting-pot for cosmic man—the world citizen. The mere format of the page of newsprint was more revolutionary in its intellectual and emotional consequences than anything that could be *said* about any part of the globe.

When we juxtapose news items from Tokyo, London, New York, Chile, Africa and New Zealand we are not just manipulating space. The events so brought together belong to cultures widely separated in time. The modern world abridges all historical times as readily as it reduces space. Every*where* and every *age* have become *here* and *now*. History has been abolished by our new media. If prehistoric man is simply preliterate man living in a timeless world of seasonal recurrence, may not posthistoric man find himself in a similar situation? May not the upshot of our technology be the awakening from the historically conditioned nightmare of the past into a timeless present? Historic man may turn out to have been literate man. An episode.

Robert Redfield in his recent book *The Primitive World and Its Transformations* points to the timeless character of preliterate societies where exclusively oral communication ensures intimacy, homogeneity and fixity of social experience. It is the advent of writing that sets in motion the urban revolution. Writing breaks up the fixity and homogeneity of preliterate societies. Writing creates that inner dialogue or dialectic, that psychic withdrawal which makes possible the reflexive analysis of thought via the stasis of the audible made spatial. Writing is the translation of the audible into the spatial as reading is the reverse of this reciprocal process. And the complex shuttling of eye, ear and speech factors once engaged in this ballet necessarily reshape the entire communal life, both inner and outer, creating not only the "stream of consciousness" rediscovered by contemporary art, but ensuring multiple impediments to the activities of perception and recall.

So far as writing is the spatializing and arrest of oral speech, however, it implies that further command of space made possible by the written message and its attendant road system. With writing, therefore, comes logical analysis and specialism, but also militarism and bureaucracy. And with writing comes the break in that direct, intuitive relationship between men and their surroundings which modern art has begun to uncover.

"Compared with the evidence afforded by living tradition," says Sir James Frazer, "the testimony of ancient books on the subject of the early religion is worth very little. For literature accelerates the advance of thought at a rate which leaves the slow progress of opinion by word of mouth at an immeasurable distance behind. Two or three generations of literature may do more to change thought than two or three thousand years of traditional life."[2] But literature, as we know today, is a relatively conservative time-binding medium compared with press, radio and movie. So the thought is now beginning to occur: How many thousands of years of change can we afford every ten years? May not a spot of culture-lag here and there in the great time-flux prove to be a kind of social and psychological oasis?

Involved with the loss of memory and the psychic withdrawal of alphabetic cultures, there is a decline of sensuous perception and adequacy of social responsiveness. The preternatural sensuous faculties of Sherlock Holmes or the modern sleuth are simply those of preliterate man who can retain the details of a hundred-mile trail as easily as a movie camera can record it. Today our detailed knowledge of societies existing within the oral tradition enables us to estimate accurately the advantages and disadvantages of writing. Without writing there is little control of space, but perfect control of accumulated experience. The misunderstandings of Ireland and England can be seen in some basic respects as the clash of oral and written cultures. And the strange thing to us is that the written culture has very little historical sense. The English could never remember; the Irish could never forget. Today the university as a community is in large degree one in which the members are in regular oral communication. And whereas the university has a highly developed time sense, the business community operates on the very short-run and exists mainly by the control of space. The present divorce between these two worlds is only accentuated by the perfection of the media peculiar to each.

Faced with the consequence of writing, Plato notes in the *Phaedrus*:

"This discovery of yours will create forgetfulness in the learners' souls, because they will not use their memories; they will trust to the external written characters and not remember of themselves. The specific which you have discovered is an aid not to memory, but to reminiscence and you give your disciples not truth but only the semblance of truth; they will be hearers of many things and have learned nothing; they will appear to be omniscient and will generally know nothing; they will be tiresome company, having the show of wisdom without the reality."

Two thousand years of manuscript culture lay ahead of the Western world when Plato made this observation. But nobody has yet studied the rise and decline of Greece in terms of the change from oral to written culture. Patrick Geddes said that the road destroyed the Greek city-state. But writing made the road possible, just as printing was later to pay for the roads of England and America.

In order to understand the printed-book culture which today is yielding, after four hundred years, to the impact of visual and auditory

media, it is helpful to note a few of the characteristics of that manuscript culture which persisted from the 5th century B.C. to the fifteenth century A.D. I shall merely mention a few of the principal
observations of scholars like Pierce Butler and H. J. Chaytor. In the
first place, manuscript culture never made a sharp break with oral
speech because everybody read manuscripts aloud. Swift, silent reading came with the macadamized surfaces of the printed page.
Manuscript readers memorized most of what they read since in the
nature of things they had to carry their learning with them. Fewness
of manuscripts and difficulty of access made for utterly different
habits of mind with regard to what was written. One result was ency-
clopedism. Men of learning tried, at least, to learn everything. So
that if learning was oral, teaching was even more so. Solitary learning
and study came only with the printed page. And today when learning
and study are switching more and more to the seminar, the round-
table and the discussion group, we have to note these developments
as due to the decline of the printed page as the dominant art form.

The manuscript page was a very flexible affair. It was not only in
close rapport with the oral speech but with plastic design and colour
illustration. So the ornate examples of manuscript art easily rival and
resemble those books in stone and glass, the cathedrals and abbeys.
In our own time James Joyce, seeking a means to orchestrate and
control the various verbi-voco-visual media of our own age, resorted
to the page format of the *Book of Kells* as a means thereto. And even
the early romantic poets, painters and novelists expressed their preference for gothic in terms of rebellion against book culture.

Recently Rosamund Tuve in elucidating the art of George Herbert
discovered that the characteristic effects of metaphysical wit in the
seventeenth-century poetry resulted from the translation of visual
effects from medieval manuscript and woodcut into the more
abstract form of the printed word. If the seventeenth century was
receding from a visual, plastic culture towards an abstract literary
culture, today we seem to be receding from an abstract book culture
towards a highly sensuous, plastic pictorial culture. Recent poets
have used simultaneously effects from both extremes to achieve witty
results not unlike those of the seventeenth century. The impact of
Mr. Eliot's very first lines of poetry has been felt everywhere:

Let us go then, you and I,
When the evening is spread out against the sky
Like a patient etherized upon a table.

It is the overlayering of perspectives, the simultaneous use of two kinds of space which creates the shock of dislocation here. For if all art is a contrived trap for the attention, all art and all language are techniques for looking at one situation through another one.

The printed page is a sixteenth-century art form which obliterated two thousand years of manuscript culture in a few decades. Yet it is hard for us to see the printed page or any other current medium except in contrast to some other form. The mechanical clock, for example, created a wholly artificial image of time as a uniform linear structure. This artificial form gradually changed habits of work, feeling and thought which are only being rejected today. We know that in our own lives each event exists in its own time. Time is not the same for the speaker as for the audience. To the speaker it is too, too brief for what he has to say. For the audience it is grim foretaste of eternity. Ultimately the medieval clock made Newtonian physics possible. It may also have initiated those orderly linear habits which made possible the rectilinear page of print created from movable type, as well as the methods of commerce. At any rate the mechanization of writing was as revolutionary in its consequences as the mechanization of time. And this, quite apart from thoughts or ideas conveyed by the printed page. Movable type was already the modern assembly line in embryo.

Harold Innis explored some of the consequences of the printed page: the break-down of international communication; the impetus given to nationalism by the commercial exploitation of vernaculars; the loss of contact between writers and audience; the depressing effect on music, architecture and the plastic arts.

Bela Balazs in his *Theory of the Film* notes some of the changes in visual habits resulting from the printing press on one hand and the camera on the other:

"The discovery of printing gradually rendered illegible the faces of men. So much could be read from paper that the method of conveying meaning by facial expression fell into desuetude. Victor Hugo wrote once that the printed book took over the part played by the cathedral in the Middle Ages and became the carrier of the spirit of the people. But the thousands of books tore the one spirit . . . into thousands of opinions . . . tore the church into a thousand books. The visual spirit was thus turned into a legible spirit and visual culture into a culture of concepts. . . . But we paid little attention to the fact that, in conformity with this, the face of individual men, their foreheads, their eyes, their mouths, had also of necessity and quite correctly to suffer a change.

At present a new discovery, a new machine is at work to turn the attention of men back to a visual culture and to give them new faces. This machine is the cinematographic camera. Like the printing press it is a technical device for the multiplication and distribution of products of the human spirit; its effect on human culture will not be less than that of the printing press. . . . The gestures of visual man are not intended to convey concepts which can be expressed in words, but such . . . non-rational emotions which would still remain unexpressed when everything that can be told has been told. . . . Just as our musical experiences cannot be expressed in rationalized concepts, what appears on the face and in facial expression is a spiritual experience which is rendered immediately visible without the intermediary of words."

The printed page in rendering the language of the face and gesture illegible has also caused the abstract media of printed words to become the main bridge for the inter-awareness of spiritual and mental states. In the epoch of print and word culture the body ceased to have much expressive value and the human spirit became audible but invisible. The camera eye has reversed this process in reacquainting the masses of men once more with the grammar of gesture. Today commerce has channelled much of this change along sex lines. But even there the power of the camera eye to change physical attitudes and make-up is familiar to all. In the nineties Oscar Wilde noted how the pale, long-necked, consumptive red-heads painted by Rossetti and Burne-Jones were for a short time an exotic visual experience. But soon in every London salon these creatures sprouted up where none had been before. The fact that human nature, at least, imitates art is too obvious to labour. But the fact that with modern technology the entire material of the globe as well as the thoughts

and feelings of its human inhabitants have become the matter of art
and of man's factive intelligence means that there is no more nature.
At least there is no more external nature. Everything from politics to
bottle-feeding, global landscape, and the subconscious of the infant is
subject to the manipulation of conscious artistic control—the BBC
carries the unrehearsed voice of the nightingale to the Congo, the
Eskimo sits entranced by hill-billy music from West Tennessee.
Under these conditions the activities of Senator McCarthy belong
with the adventures of the Pickwick Club and our talk about the Iron
Curtain is a convenient smoke-screen likely to divert our attention
from much greater problems. The Russians differ from us in being
much more aware of the non-commercial impact of the new media.
We have been so hypnotized with the commercial and entertainment
qualities of press, radio, movie and TV that we have been blind to the
revolutionary character of these toys. The Russians after a few years
of playing with these radio-active toys have tried to neutralize them
by imposing various stereotypes on their content and messages. They
have forced their press to stick to an 1850 format. They have
imposed similar time-locks on music and literature. They hope,
thereby, to abate the revolutionary fury of these instruments. But the
fury for change is in the form and not the message of the new media,
a fact which seems almost inevitably to escape men trained in our
abstract literary culture. The culture of print has rendered people
extremely insensitive to the language and meaning of spatial forms—
one reason for the architectural and city horrors tolerated by pre-
dominantly book-cultures. Thus the English and American cultures
in particular were overwhelmed by print, since in the sixteenth century they had only rudimentary defences to set up against the new
printed word. The rest of Europe, richer in plastic and oral culture,
was less blitzed by the printing press. And the Orient has so far had
many kinds of resistance to offer. But the curious thing is that
Spaniards like Picasso or Salvador Dali are much more at home
amidst the new visual culture of North America than we ourselves.

This division between visual and literary languages is a fact which has
also set a great abyss between science and the humanities. Thinking
as we do of culture in book terms, we are unable to read the language
of technological forms. And since our earliest esthetic responses are

to such forms, this has set up numerous cleavages between official and idiomatic cultural response within our own experience. We are all of us persons of divided and sub-divided sensibility through failure to recognize the multiple languages with which our world speaks to us. Above all it is the multiplicity of messages with which we are hourly bombarded by our environment that renders us ineffectual. Karl Deutsch has argued that a people shaped by oral tradition will respond to an alien challenge like a suicidal torpedo. The wild Celtic charge. A people shaped by a written tradition will not charge, but drift, pulled in a thousand different directions.

One obvious feature of the printed book is its republicanism. The page of print is not only a leveller of other forms of expression; it is a social leveller as well. Anyone who can read has at least the illusion of associating on equal terms with anyone who has written. And that fact gave the printed word a privileged place in American society and politics. The Duke of Gloucester could say casually to Edward Gibbon, on the completion of his *History*: "Another damned fat square book. Scribble, scribble, scribble, eh, Mr. Gibbon!" But there were no fox-hunters in America to put the literary upstart in his place.

So far as quantity goes the printed book was the first instrument of mass culture. Erasmus was the first to see its meaning and turned his genius to the manufacture of textbooks for the classroom. He saw, above all, that the printing press was a device for reproducing the past in the present, much like a Hollywood movie set. The *nouveaux riches* of Italy began to enact on a tiny scale the past that was being unearthed and printed. Hastily they ran up villas and palazzas in ancient style. Assisted by the newly printed exemplars they began to imitate the language of Cicero and Seneca. In England the new print mingled with the old oral tradition to produce the new forms of sermon and drama which were hybrids of written and spoken culture. But in the printing press there is one great feature of mass culture which is lacking. Namely, the instantaneous. From one point of view, language itself is the greatest of all mass media. The spoken word instantly evokes not only some recently conceived idea but reverberates with the total history of its own experience with man. We may be oblivious of such overtones as of the spectrum of colour in a lump of coal. But the poet by exact rhythmic adjustment can flood our consciousness with this knowledge. The artist is older than the fish.

Reading the history of the newspaper restrospectively we can see that it was not a mere extension of the art form of the book page. As used by Rimbaud, Mallarmé and Joyce the newspaper page is a revolution in itself, juxtaposing many book pages on a single sheet. And the news page was, moreover, more nearly a mass medium not only in reaching more people than the book, but in being more instantaneous in its coverage and communication. Once linked to the telegraph, the press achieved the speed of light, as radio and TV have done since then. Total global coverage in space, instantaneity in time. Those are the two basic characters that I can detect in a mechanical mass medium. There are other characteristics derivative from these, namely anonymity of those originating the messages or forms, and anonymity in the recipients. But in respect of this anonymity it is necessary to regard not only words and metaphors as mass media but buildings and cities as well.

The modern newspaper page is not a mere extension of the book page because the speed with which the telegraph feeds news to the press today precludes any possibility of organizing a sheet of news by any but the most impressionistic devices. Each item lives in its own kind of space totally discontinuous from all other items. A particularly vigorous item will sprout a headline and provide a kind of aura or theme for surrounding items. So that, if the book page could imitate visual perspective as in Renaissance painting, setting facts and concepts in proportions that reproduced the optical image of the three-dimensional object-world, the uninhibited world of the press and modern advertising abandoned such realistic proprieties in favor of weighting news and commercial objects by every dynamic and structural device of size and colour bringing words and pictures back into a plastic and meaningful connection. If the book page tends to perspective, the news page tends to cubism and surrealism. So that every page of newspapers and magazines, like every section of our cities, is a jungle of multiple, simultaneous perspectives which make the world of hot jazz and bebop seem relatively sedate and classical. Our intellectual world, by virtue of the same proliferation of books (over 18,000 new titles in England alone last year) has achieved the same entanglement which is easier to assess through the complexity of our visual environment. It is not just a quantitative problem, of course. As Gyorgy Kepes states it in his *Language of Vision*:

"The environment of man living today has a complexity which cannot be compared with any environment of any previous age. The skyscrapers, the street with its kaleidoscopic vibration of colors, the window-displays with their multiple mirroring images, the street cars and motor cars, produce a dynamic simultaneity of visual impression which cannot be perceived in the terms of inherited visual habits. In this optical turmoil the fixed objects appear utterly insufficient as the measuring tape of the events. The artificial light, the flashing of electric bulbs, and the mobile game of the many new types of light-sources bombard man with kinetic colour sensations having a keyboard never before experienced. Man, the spectator, is himself more mobile than ever before. He rides in streetcars, motorcars and aeroplanes and his own motion gives to optical impacts a tempo far beyond the threshold of a clear object-perception. The machine man operates adds its own demand for a new way of seeing. The complicated interactions of its mechanical parts cannot be conceived in a static way; they must be perceived by understanding of their movements. The motion picture, television, and, in a great degree, the radio, require a new thinking, i.e., seeing, that takes into account qualities of change, interpenetration and simultaneity."

That situation can be snapshotted from many angles. But it always adds up to the need to discover means for translating the experience of one medium or one culture into another, of translating Confucius into Western terms and Kant into Eastern terms. Of seeing our old literary culture in the new plastic terms in order to enable it to become a constitutive part of the new culture created by the orchestral voices and gestures of new media. Of seeing that modern physics and painting and poetry speak a common language and of acquiring that language at once in order that our world may possess consciously the coherence that it really has in latency, and which for lack of our recognition has created not new orchestral harmonies but mere noise.

Perhaps the terrifying thing about the new media for most of us is their inevitable evocation of irrational response. The irrational has become the major dimension of experience in our world. And yet this is a mere by-product of the instantaneous character in communication. It can be brought under rational control. It is the perfection of the means which has so far defeated the end, and removed the time necessary for assimilation and reflection. We are now compelled to develop new techniques of perception and judgement, new ways of reading the languages of our environment with its multiplicity of cultures and disciplines. And these needs are not just desperate remedies but roads to unimagined cultural enrichment.

All the types of linear approach to situations past, present or future are useless. Already in the sciences there is recognition of the need for a unified field theory which would enable scientists to use one continuous set of terms by way of relating the various scientific universes. Thus the basic requirement of any system of communication is that it be circular, with, of course, the possibility of self-correction. That is why presumably the human dialogue is and must ever be the basic form of all civilization. For the dialogue compels each participant to see and recreate his own vision through another sensibility. And the radical imperfection in mechanical media is that they are not circular. So far they have become one-way affairs with audience research taking the place of the genuine human vision, heckling and response. There is not only the anonymity of press, movies and radio but the factor of scale. The individual cannot discuss a problem with a huge, mindless bureaucracy like a movie studio or a radio corporation. On the other hand a figure like Roosevelt could mobilize the networks for a war with the press. He could even make the microphone more effective by having the press against him, because the intimacy of the microphone preserved his human dimension while the national scale of the press attack could only appear as a tank corps converging on a telephone booth.

Thus the microphone invites chat, not oratory. It is a new art form which transforms all the existing relations between speakers and their audiences and speakers and their material of discourse. "The great rhetorical tradition which begins with Halifax and runs through Pitt to Channing, sent up its expiring flash in Macaulay."[3] The modern manner was less declamatory and more closely reasoned. And the new manner which Gladstone handled like a Tenth Muse was based on facts and figures. Statistics represents a branch of pictorial expression. If the rise of bureaucracy and finance changed the style of public and private speech, how much more radical a change is daily worked in our habits of thought and discourse by the microphone and the loudspeaker.

Perhaps we could sum up our problem by saying that technological man must betake himself to visual metaphor in contriving a new unified language for the multiverse of cultures of the entire globe. All language or expression is metaphorical because metaphor is the seeing of one situation through another one. Right on the beam. I'll take a rain check on that.

One's vernacular is best seen and felt through another tongue. And for us, at least, society is only appreciated by comparing and contrasting it with others. Pictorial and other experience today is filled with metaphors from all the cultures of the globe. Whereas the written vernaculars have always locked men up within their own cultural monad, the language of technological man, while drawing on all the cultures of the world, will necessarily prefer those media which are least national. The language of visual form is, therefore, one which lies to hand as an unused Esperanto at everybody's command. The language of vision has already been adopted in the pictograms of scientific formula and logistics. These ideograms transcend national barriers as easily as Chaplin or Disney and would seem to have no rivals as the cultural base for cosmic man.

MICHEL A. MOOS

McLuhan's Language for Awareness
under Electronic Conditions

McLuhan's Language for Awareness under Electronic Conditions

*T*n the wake of the publication of *Understanding Media* in the summer of 1964, the *New York Herald Tribune* rated its author "the most important thinker since Newton, Darwin, Freud, Einstein, and Pavlov. . . ." Transformed overnight from an English professor with an interest in technology to haruspex laureate of the Information Age, during the next years Marshall McLuhan found himself a high-profile *figure* of the media networks whose hidden *ground* he had so carefully analyzed. The challenge of McLuhan's insight into the cultural revolution provoked by electricity was met as best it could be, perhaps, generating a fanfare and a hoopla somewhat proportionate to the magnitude of its impact. On one hand, this was fortunate, for the timeliness of acute relevance can often induce indifference. On the other hand, however, this is largely what happened; in the excitement that his revelations provoked, the brunt of McLuhan's message was more absorbed than assimilated, rather more regurgitated than digested. Just when McLuhan predicted packages would be obsolete, he himself was being packaged in a manner which ensured that the implications of what he was saying would be deflected, diffused, and deferred, filed with playful bewilderment alongside the unfathomable contributions of other "geniuses." If "$E = MC^2$" and the Theory of Relativity reminded us that Einstein had redefined the nature of the universe, catchphrases like "the medium is the message" and "global village" told us the new Einstein of communications theory, Marshall McLuhan, had, with a similarly baffling command of counterintuition, redefined our world and the nature of everything we do in it. If, as Lewis Lapham recently noted, "Much of what McLuhan had to say makes a good deal more sense in 1994 than it did in 1964," it is probably equally true today, as Tom Wolfe remarked in the sixties, that "McLuhan is one of those intellectual celebrities, like Toynbee or Einstein, who is intensely well known as a name, and as a *savant*, while his theory remains a grand blur."[1]

The problem of McLuhan's reception begins with the business of reading him. If the resistance posed by Einstein's work is relatively straightforward—demonstrations and proofs expressed in the abstract formulae of an esoteric notation—the difficulty McLuhan's ideas present is somewhat more perplexing. McLuhan's books are not only written in English by an English professor with sterling credentials, but by one who had opted to shed the recondite posturing of academic prose in favor of a more colloquial, exoteric delivery. Never, it would seem, had intent and effect been better mismatched. To hear tell of it from critics who wager a repeated charge of coruscated abstrusity, the work in question might just as well be James Joyce's *Finnegans Wake*, where it *can* be argued that accessibility is impaired by a novel style of grammatical and syntactical aphasia. Hyperbolic detraction aside, however, it appears that where the ideas in McLuhan's writings are hard to grasp, it has something to do with the writing itself being, on some literal level, hard to read. Curiously, as reader experience often attests, this literal impedence lies less in deciphering the thoughts on McLuhan's page than in limiting the effects these thoughts have in the reader's own head. The editor of a prominent art magazine told me he had taken up reading McLuhan *again* for the first time. After countless false starts, he was resolutely forging his way through *Understanding Media*, about five pages at a time. When I asked why he read so few pages per evening, he said that if he allowed himself to read more, he couldn't sleep. Similarly, in a recent course a student of mine wrote: "Marshall McLuhan is a master of the language. His intellectual capacity makes my mind explode. I have to keep re-reading this stuff in order to soak in everything, but there's still stuff that I still don't get. I began reading *War and Peace in the Global Village*, and I had to put the book down because I was like, 'What is this guy saying?' McLuhan might speak English, but someone needs to translate it for me!" Such accounts suggest McLuhan's writing is not so much hard to read as it is hard to keep reading, so hard in fact that not reading him at length has become the sanctioned approach in an age of attention deficits. "Reading

McLuhan continuously is not a good idea," contends Derrick de Kerckhove, director of the McLuhan Program in Culture and Technology at the University of Toronto, located in the little coach house from which McLuhan once operated. "It's better to jump in, take a peek, and then go somewhere with it." And the reporter quoting him reasons in conclusion: "So maybe we don't need to read McLuhan cover to cover, but only in probe-length bits, while savouring the stinging effects of these viruses of the mind. Perhaps McLuhan has joined the small elite of pivotal thinkers whose lessons have entered general consciousness."[2] General consciousness or grand blur, the problem is that McLuhan's probes do not have a specific length. Many of his sentences are ready-made probes, terse and often ingenious aphorisms. They frequently occur as a cluster of two or three sentences or phrases, and as a unit the probe expands to the length of the essay, the book, and beyond. Unlike monotone "point of view" prose that can only proceed along a single level of analysis, McLuhan's probe prose is a studied response to the challenge of at all capturing in writing the paradoxical logic and complexity that is our lot in an age of electronic information processing. This "cubist prose" is deliberately assembled with a degree of interpenetration and simultaneous multilevel montage such as is foreign to the one-thing-at-a-time sensibility of print. As an inclusive and infinitely rescalable artifact, the probe is therefore less a discrete reading unit (like the paragraph) than it is a technique of articulation and insight into the complex life of media forms. For those accustomed to equi-tone "Mandarin prose" which confines analysis at all times to a single level and form, McLuhan's writing probably remains as bewildering as the multimedia *infoscape* it describes. Yet McLuhan not only considers this multilayered prose a "serious art form," but a necessary mutation if serious critical analysis is to keep pace with the increasing complexity of the object it purports to describe.[3]

The construction of McLuhan's work therefore naturally raises the deconstructive question of hypertextuality. The dream of key words and patterns functioning as quasi-magical entrances to a networked reality is nothing new; what is new is the use of electricity to transform the archive of knowledge into a transparent labyrinth. One recalls Vannevar Bush's description of his Memex machine in the forties, a sort of editing desk for microfilm with elaborate

spool-switching capacities.[4] There is Theodor Nelson's Xanadu project which continues to languish somewhere between the market-
place and the location from which it takes its name. It was Nelson
who coined the word *hypertext* in 1965 when he called for a comput-
erized text system based on "nonsequential writing" that would allow
students to explore academic material along a variety of alternate
paths. Envisioned as a tremendously souped-up word processing
interface, even by today's standards, Xanadu "was meant to be a universal library, a world-wide publishing tool, a system to resolve copyright disputes, and a meritocratic forum for discussion and debate."[5]
Similarly in *S/Z*, Roland Barthes assigns literature the task of making
the reader no longer the consumer but the producer of text, and
speculates upon the characteristics of an open-ended, infinitely
branching network of *lexia* or text blocks:

> In this ideal text, the networks are many and interact, without any one of
> them being able to surpass the rest; this text is a galaxy of signifiers, not a
> structure of signifieds; it has no beginning; it is reversible; we gain access
> to it by several entrances, none of which can be authoritatively declared
> to be the main one . . . systems of meaning can take over this absolutely
> plural text, but their number is never closed, based as it is on the infinity
> of language.[6]

Still more recently, as the computer implementation of this ideal,
hypertext has been heralded as the testing ground for, if not the realization of, various claims of structuralist and poststructuralist criticism. Issues concerning textuality, narrative, and reader/writer
functionality dealt with by theorists as diverse as Barthes, Bakhtin,
Derrida, and Foucault, can apparently find resolution in the instru-
mentalization of an interactive, screen-based environment of textual
exchange: "Using hypertext, critical theorists will have, or now
already have, a new laboratory, in addition to the conventional
library of printed texts, in which to test their ideas."[7]

As conceptualized here, hypertext represents a technological
response to the effects of electricity on the verbal organization of
knowledge. In this sense, the development of hypertext is governed
by the programming thresholds of the computer and is currently
implemented in text and image software applications and in the
browsing and search agents of the World Wide Web. Yet in the gap
that exists between the textual model of the book and the hypercon-

nectivity of electric circuits, the future of a specific mode of think-ing-in-language hangs in the balance, that mode of thought pro-cessing we associate with reading and the outlook afforded by literacy. As McLuhan puts it in "Culture Without Literacy": "Historic man may turn out to have been literate man. An episode." At this juncture of text's going hyper—of language leaving the page for the screen—McLuhan's work provides a valuable alternative route to what may otherwise prove to be the irrelevance of verbal discourse as we know it.

For in the transparent translation of text from page to screen that poststructuralism imagines, in the migration of testable and therefore unaltered ideas excised from their medium of expression, no account has been taken of what happens to the "train of thought" that makes these texts and these ideas possible. Conformant with originary structuralist hyperbole that sees every-thing as a certain kind of language and this language itself as infi-nite, the poststructuralist vision of hypertextuality blindly embraces the site of obliteration of the specific kind of language that it speaks. It should be obvious in an infinitely recombinant textuality which allows for continual splicing and intercutting between any and all documents and text fragments, as well as other audiovisual data, that the first thing to disappear is the specific density or "voice" of thought that exists only as the fictionally seamless col-lage you are presently reading. With theoretical claims to hyper-text, a certain kind of discourse sets out to take all of culture as its object without noticing that electricity radically alters the architec-ture of language's response time to thought. In McLuhan's terms, this wholesale projection of typographic discursive practices into electrographic form is a classic case of the "rearview mirror view": seeing in the form of a new technology simply a novel way of doing more of what the old technology did. Hence the wishful contention that the new electronic space be merely another archive, an addi-tive, identic annex to the conventional library of print, so the work of testing ideas may remain that of embedding them in the system of reference that constitutes print's technology of storage and retrieval. Yet as McLuhan understands, if "computers are being asked to do things that belong to the old technology" the onus of survival rests not with computers but with book consciousness or what Robert Romanyshyn calls "ego-ocular-verbocentrism."[8] The question of the implementation of hypertext is, at base, this question of the survival of literate values and practices. By way of updating McLuhan's admonition that "the values of the Gutenberg era cannot be salvaged by those who are as unaware of how they came into existence as they are of why they are now in the process of liquidation,"[9] one might note that McLuhan answers the question of hypertext's implementation by showing both how language is already a hypermedium and how the future of textual discourse depends on recognizing and exploiting language's own technical limitations and finite essence.

To view McLuhan's writing as hypertext is to see how textual discursivity can branch out and interconnect with other media and other forms of information while still being what it is: analytic thought recorded in writing for the reader to follow. Understood as the jolt one gets from reading him, the hypertextuality of McLuhan's "mosaic" approach stems in large part from the fact that he is necessarily engaged in performing two jobs at once: making sense of "the ways of thinking implanted by electronic culture" and, in order to do so, debunking "those fostered by print culture."[10] At the same time as discussing the nature and properties of all media, he defends against fallout from the medium he is using, against the short-circuit of awareness that occurs when the medium itself has already become message, has subliminally been allowed to dictate the horizon of meaning's possibility, to modulate primary experience. By consistently sending or drawing attention to the source code of the book's program together with the message or meaning encoded therein, the reader is debriefed as he proceeds. These twinned concerns may be said to function as the systole and diastole of McLuhan's thought, each new insight or probe being sent out with the means for descrambling its own bias or source code. In McLuhan's terms, feed*forward* depends on understanding the nature of the feedback one is generating. Thus the retooling of literary studies *for* media analysis first involves the media analysis *of* literary studies. In this respect, McLuhan's preoccupation with the reading code accounts for much of the perceived difficulty in reading him; it is also this aspect of his work dealing with the renovation of critical discourse in terms of a postliterate discursivity that contextualizes McLuhan vis-à-vis poststructuralism and deconstruction.

The question of McLuhan's tangential relationship to poststructuralism is incisively adumbrated by the recent studies of Friedrich Kittler, notably his *Discourse Networks, 1800/1900*. As an "heir to McLuhan's legacy," Kittler here provides what may well be considered a *Gutenberg Galaxy* for poststructuralists.[11] For literary critics still floundering in the hermeneutic jungle of meanings either overgrown or partially exfoliated by the French poststructural triumvirate (Foucault, Derrida, Lacan)—depending on how one looks at it— Kittler's genealogy of readership is a heady and incontrovertible antidote. In applying McLuhan's medial definition of language as interactive product of technological thresholds not to media *per se* but to discourse itself, Kittler concretizes with brutal facticity the materially specific historical determinisms that remain merely thematic surface adaptations in poststructuralism. The notion of two discourse networks is slightly misleading; insofar as discourse refers to the totality of alphabetically induced, stored and recorded thought there is only one discourse network. Yet intradiscursive mutation between 1800 and 1900 is so marked that discourse itself gives the impression of two distinct realms of culture and thought. The dividing line is the collapse of "Gutenberg's storage monopoly" around 1880 when machines now "conquer functions of the central nervous system, not merely the muscular system as they did previously."[12] With the advent of electricity, the precise physiological coordination of eye, ear, hand and inner voice that represented alphabetism's technological lock on information processing is superseded, and the book no longer administers all serial data flows. The rise of psychophysics and the development of machines for transcribing mental output in real time drastically relativizes the entire apparatus of writing surrounding the book, which is now just one recording technology among many amidst a growing spectrum of "partially connected media systems."[13] The literary disciplines poetry and philosophy that once "were on the technological cutting edge because more than any others they could speak to and exploit alphabetized bodies,"[14] witnessed the breakup of this body as its sensory outputs were committed to technological data storages that overrode (and overwrote) the cogito of the reading subject. But in highlighting the implications of this inevitability for literature, as his study of its discursive net before (1800) and after (1900) does, the thrust of Kittler's analysis is to issue an ultimatum for human sciences and for literary criticism: either interconnect medially or begin to de-exist in terms of relevance. As Kittler recounts:

> They [the students at Stanford] asked me what I thought about the theory of relativity. Since I didn't know a thing about relativity, I went to the library and started reading. I noticed then that the technological transformation of what we know, in terms of literary science, is the only thing that can be transmitted and, in fact, comes across, indeed, justifiably comes across, because literary science, in short, means translating and applying the structures of the Gutenberg age to those of the electronic age.[15]

If structuralism and poststructuralism both finally describe belea-guered attempts of a "literate" criticism to proceed as "hard science," here, within the covers of the present volume or the pages of *Discourse Networks*, is a rigorous and successful demonstration of how to go about it.

Where hypertext in all its forms is the challenge for writing to develop medial interfaces with other technological media, the question behind the implementation of hypertext is in essence that of language's connection to the world. In poststructural terms, this challenge became represented as the attempt to get *outside* language. In this respect, poststructuralism's version of hypertext follows Foucault's "thinking of the outside," the thinking of language as a domain recalcitrant to internalization. Yet the prospect of treating discourses "in terms not of the gentle, silent, intimate consciousness that is expressed in them, but of an obscure set of anonymous rules,"[16] was finally for Foucault the subject of an admirable hesita-tion; discursive rules remain intelligible with the result that Foucault overlooks technologies. Thus in that "reappearance of language as a multiple profusion" Foucault sees as marking the disappearance of unitary discourse,[17] he fails to notice that these multiple dialects *are* the technological thresholds of new media. Crucially, of course, this is because Foucault overlooks the material properties of the very technology he is using: that of the language of print. In its resultant conflation of language with thought, it is an oversight that identifies more generally postmodernism's symptomatic belatedness. Where modernity *was* the development of technological media that broke the book's monopoly on classical thought, this was already a technogical inevitability *external* to language itself. In this sense deconstructive postmodernism predates modernism where it fails finally to question the operational grammar of typographic inscription which alone is responsible for this infinite coextensivity of Man and Discourse that hallmarks the classical order.

Perhaps the best way of putting this is to say that from the particular perspective of typographic literacy, there are two outsides: one of which is internal to language but external to a way of thinking based in the technological properties of print; and the other which is external both to print and to language itself. The postmodern book has conflated these two outsides so that thinking the real *beyond* of language has become utterly confused with the task of first excavating the interiority of typographic literacy in relation to language itself. Insofar as it still neglects to perform this latter task of considering the discursive rules of print at the level of their material deployment (prior, as it were, to questions of meaning and intelligibility), postmodern literary discourse merely withdraws further into the double interiority of this regrettable quixotic inversion that posits everything in terms of the "literary bias."[18] It is the sort of dry conceit that forces a critic like Paul de Man to retreat from the difficulty of "concise theoretical exposition" into "a pragmatic discourse"— which means illustrating his point with "a few specific textual examples" taken "from the sub-literature of the mass media"—in this case, a television sitcom.[19] The configuration is as obvious as it is overlooked and the implication embarrassingly clear: the world is still a book, poststructural literary theory sees "language" as an infinite text, and all forms of communication are contained in and derivable from Literature. On this account, we are still at the Kantian zenith of a transcendental hermeneutics whose presupposition of intelligibility was a myth for the print reader's silent inner voice, whose individual universal *was* typography's construction of a philosophy for its reading subject. "The traumatic shock of moving from the segmental, lineal space of literacy into the auditory, unified field of electronic information"[20] is for academic denizens of the book much like seeing the light was for the blinkered inmates of Plato's proverbial cave: they continue to "believe that what was seen before is truer than what is now shown" so that the mass media actually go on appearing as so many literary subforms.[21] In the face of such apotropaic luddism shielding the mental habits of the book from the absolute danger posed to it by the forces of modernity, it is plain to see how McLuhan's diagnosis remains anathema within the precincts of literary criticism. Rather than confront, as McLuhan does, the "crazy mosaic of contradictions" and "contradictory polarities" of a world where "ordinary consciousness is exposed to the patternmaking of several media at once," the literate-minded find it preferable to maintain a view through "literary lenses" at all costs, colonially granting a pattern of literate consciousness to all media.[22]

Such retrofitted expansionism explains why for the poststructural hypertextualists there is no difference between hypertext and hypermedia. Without ever emerging from the interiority of a print-conditioned consciousness, poststructural hypertext envisages an information medium linking verbal and nonverbal media according to the same modality that textual information alone can be interconnected. On the one hand, hyper*text* would already denote an information medium linking verbal and nonverbal information while, on the other hand, hyper*media* would simply extend the notion of the text in hypertext beyond the solely verbal.[23] That mass literacy, like all mass media, inevitably imposes its own culture-script upon us seems as alien to the literate as the realization that literacy is itself a mass medium. To take printed texts as a paradigmatic hypermedial web of interconnected materials is merely to extend the ideology of mass literacy to all media. This is like taking a horseless carriage approach to the automobile or a power-book view of computing.

In many ways, William Gibson's book *Neuromancer* is a deft parable of ensuing limitations imposed by a viewpoint of hyperliteracy. Initially a psychology of alphabetization created by the automatized coupling of reading and writing via a singular kind of listening ("the mental sound movie which we call reading"[24]), the site of Romanticism's hypnotic intoxication is replayed as "Cyberspace. A consensual hallucination experienced daily by billions of legitimate operators, in every nation. . . . A graphic representation of data abstracted from the banks of every computer in the human system. Unthinkable complexity." The process whereby a graphic representation of data is abstracted from every human computer refers to mass literacy itself as a program for universal education, the legitimate operators being so many people schooled into reading and writing

individuals. Like printed communication and experience, the cyberspace matrix comes alive as a consensual hallucination by forgetting
that it is "actually a drastic simplification of the human sensorium."[25]
Cyberspace, in other words, rehearses a literalized version of the cinematic process of introjection that is the internalized end product of
literacy; participation in an "audiovisual hallucination" that "exists
only as the inner possession of senses that are dead to the world."[26]
When the book's neoromantic hero, Case, finally hacks into the data
core and draws back the curtain of cyberspatial Oz, the artificially
intelligent operating system generating this virtual world's matrix
appears to him in the guise of the old man Finn and divulges: "Minds
aren't *read*. See, you've still got the paradigms print gave you, and
you're barely print-literate. I can *access* your memory, but that's not
the same as your mind."[27] Where the romantic imagination was
alphabetization-made-flesh, the consensual hallucination promised
by cyberspace threatens to be no more than alphabetization *electro-
dally* implanted. The ability to recognize and imagine oneself into a
hypermedium or cybernetic space depends precisely upon divesting
oneself of cognitive habits instilled by the mind-set of print. As imagined by postructural literati, hypermedia—or cyberspace—is in danger of becoming no more than hypertext, no more than an automated
archive, an online data-bank of recorded and reified experience—
experience captured by and reduced to linear thinking.

McLuhan's prescient assessment of a hypermedial future for textuality lies in the intricate awareness first of text's relationship to language, and second of the forces responsible for the arrangement of
language by thought processes or experience. It is no coincidence in
this regard that the road to *Understanding Media* is paved with work
done in *The Gutenberg Galaxy: The Making of Typographic Man*.
Intended "to trace the ways in which the *forms* of experience and of
mental outlook and expression have been modified, first by the phonetic alphabet and then by printing,"[28] the *Galaxy*'s methodology
propels McLuhan astutely into the multimedia landscape because it
treats literacy as a technological extension of language. This understanding of literacy and language to be closed systems, analyzable as
historically finite resources dependent upon material conditions and
supports, preemptively fulfills postmodern structuralism's agenda to
provide a positive description of textuality's effect and operation

from the standpoint of the user. It explains how from the outset the structuralist enterprise mistakes its own local aims for a universal mandate to equate man with language ("*Qui dit homme, dit langage,*" as Lévi-Strauss surmised): language can be imagined as infinite, as coextensive with conscious (and unconscious) thought, only where it has become the subject of technological cathexis, a projection or extension of a part of ourselves invested with enough collective attention to dictate behavior to the whole of ourselves. Textual literacy is this technological extension of language, the outering of language via typographic inscription and its concomitant reinternalization as express simulacrum of real-time speech through the rote practice of silent reading. Literate individuals tend to acquire an ingrained habit of hearing themselves think, of forming their thoughts in a tone that comes to seem as natural as the way one talks to oneself. It is through the persistence of this interior monologue, which runs on in readers' heads even when they do not have printed text before them, that mass literacy indelibly shapes all aspects of a culture in which it has been heavily instituted. Realizing this requires looking at a medium in terms of its interface, describing it from the outside—i. e., according to how it works—something for which McLuhan retains a vivid ability. Hence he pinpoints the characteristic feel of the text medium as the specific way of relating to the particular effect that it creates:

> Yet printing is itself just such a camera obscura, yielding a private vision of the movements of others. While sitting in the dark, one has in the camera obscura a cinematic presentation of the outside world. And in reading print, the reader acts as a kind of projector of the still shots or printed words, which he can read fast enough to have the feeling of re-creating the movements of another mind. Manuscripts could not be read at a speed sufficient to create the sense of a mind actively engaged in learning and in self-expression.

In other words, recalling the distinction made by Gibson's cyberspatial entity, print supplies the illusion of *mind reading*; it creates the sensation that one is "sharing the movements of another mind," when in fact the print-reader is only *accessing a memory*, a record of experience.[29]

If the experience of print is, technically, someone else's déjà vu recalled, what sets McLuhan's description apart is his underlying definition of communication as an assemblage or montage of consciousness. Media can only be described when contrasted with one another because information is a function of *relative speeds of perception*.[30] The properties of a medium therefore lie less in the isolated functions of its message (Shannon's source, sender, channel, receiver, and drain of information streams) than in the overall form of perception the means of communication *de facto* confers upon any message. The network of information or pattern of communication of a medium effects a fixed displacement of the assemblage point of experience itself: the seat of the montage.[31] With print, the seat of the montage is in the perception of the spectator—the reader. Such awareness radically qualifies the much-touted postmodern claim that hypertext is the medium that will transform passive reader into active writing subject. Decrying the harsh divorce the literary institution maintains between the makers and the users of text, between owner and client, author and reader, Barthes for example singles out text's "readerliness" (*le lisible*) as its negative value and "writerliness" (*le scriptible*) as its positive value, positing literature's endeavor as that of graduating the reader from consumer to producer of text.[32] For postmodern hypertextualists, hypertext—"text that branches and allows choices to the reader, best read at an interactive screen"[33]—provides the medium for the merger of reader with writer because it purportedly "offers the reader and writer the same environment," namely that of "the text-processing program."[34] Yet to confound the experience of the reader with the experience of the writer is to reiterate an old paradigm, not conceive a new one. When William Paulson says, "What literature solicits of the reader is not simply reception but the active, independent, autonomous construction of meaning,"[35] he is saying that *reading creates* "the sense of a mind actively engaged in learning and in self-expression." But this is a special effect created in the perception of the reader, not a general condition of texts or writers. Literate text is, by definition, read-only memory. Its rich sense of an autonomous, random-access memory at work exists solely during the reader's *spectation* of an arrangement of thought. Reading is what *runs* the text-processing program of printed matter and print culture. One writes, in other words, not merely as one thinks—i.e., randomly and freely—but as one reads, that is, in essence, sequentially, lineally. To assume the authoring function—to become a print programmer—is to become conformed in writing to a mode of thought whose meaning has been optimized for the perception of the reader. Thus authorship in the discourse network of print "is not a function simultaneous with the act of writing, but a deferred effect of rereading."[36] Looking to the model of the author for the liberation of the reader merely reenacts this fiction—in the root plastic sense of making (*fingere*)—of the literary form, namely, that literacy has no write-only mode in the sense of simultaneous or real-time apprehension of thought processes. When the postmodern hypertextualists imagine that, "With the advent of hypertext, it has become possible to move among related areas of information with a speed and flexibility that at least approach finally accommodating the workings of human intellect,"[37] inadvertently they are restating the operation of the print processor's instruction set. Were they to investigate the matter of print's technical processing limitations, they would have realized that in terms of the thought structures text is capable of conveying, the literary form is a *hypo*medium, and already tends more towards *hypo*text in having "eliminated most language and speech from its medium."[38]

The question behind the question of hypertext's implementation is therefore one of understanding what it is that the *hyper* in hypertext stands for or refers to. When we say in this way that text processed electronically will give us *more*, more of *what*, exactly, in text is implied? McLuhan's approach to media starts with this question because it begins by accounting for how it is that media come to function as drastic simplifications of the human sensorium. Examined from inside the five sense sensorium, media tend to isolate one or another sense from the others and dilate that sense to fill the whole field, creating conditions of anesthesia or hypnosis in that area. The effects of literacy constitute a case study of this process, for if "the formula for hypnosis is 'one sense at a time,'" literacy "stresses lineality, a one-thing-at-a-time awareness and mode of procedure."[39] Hence the characteristic absent- (or "abced-") mindedness, "the loss of memory and the psychic withdrawal of alphabetic cultures" which in acquiring the "phoney habit" (as Joyce puts it), experience "decline of sensuous perception and adequacy of social responsiveness."[40] Taking all of our technologies to be ablations of our faculties, McLuhan "reads" literacy like any mechanical technology that is an extension of physical organs, namely, the organs of speech. As "an

immediate technological extension of the human person" print gives
the literate individual a virtual body of thought whose sense of self or
outline conforms him to the "assumptions latent in typographic segmentation."[41] These assumptions are chiefly those of visual space and
order, and to the extent that a self constituted via literacy is one conditioned to apprehend and express thought through speech analyzed
for the eye, the literate individual inhabits this visual space the pre-
conceptions of which isolate him from his other senses:

> Visual space has peculiar properties that are not shared by any of the
> other senses. Visual space is continuous, uniform, connected and static,
> whereas the sense of touch, like the sense of hearing or smell, is
> discontinuous, disconnected, non-uniform and dynamic. Such is also
> the case with acoustic space, the space in which we all live in the
> electric age.[42]

Zeno's paradox is an early expression of this awareness that only
visual space can be divided and as such is a suspension of tactility, tactility being not a sense but an interplay of all the senses.[43] The phonetic alphabet inaugurates purely visual thinking because it begins to
circumvent the ear; the techniques inherent in the visual organization and application of knowledge become fully realized when typography silences the ear altogether by making silent reading possible.
Yet the crux of the matter has to do with the fact that although we
think of vision as the fastest, most immediate sense, to process language visually leads to an extremely slowed-down thought process,
an almost static arrest of mental motion. When "literacy gave us an
eye for an ear"[44] it reduced language from a dialogue to an interior
monologue, that portion of speech that trickles through to your ear
when it has been converted to a surrogate eye, so that "thinking itself,
for the literate person, is primarily structuring speech in the silence
of one's mind."[45] Literate listening is a highly trained kind of visual
thinking. This conforming of thought to speech rather than the use
of speech as we may think tends to siphon off most of the interactive
alacrity germane to spoken forms of awareness, so that the story of
print culture's hegemonic visual lock on language can be told as the
strip-mining of language's own telluric resources. Where in relation
to oral cultures literacy can be said to accelerate the advance of
thought at a rate responsible for conjuring the very notion of
progress, at electric speeds of interdependence the monorails of lit-

erate thinking are felt to place an unbearable bottleneck on the speed of movement of thought itself. Paradoxically, literate isolation of sense interplay is also a kind of shortsightedness in that it obscures that "which is rendered immediately visible without the intermediary of words."[46]

The first move towards a hypermedium in the sense intended by hypertext would therefore be to effect a reentry into language by looking to the model of oral dialogue as a medium more conducive to providing the user with an environment in which he is free to make associations and connections as they occur to him. It is in this sense that McLuhan's discursive style of "academic free association"[47] perhaps best instantiates the sort of hypertextual experience the literary hypertextualists are dreaming of. The form his argumentation takes, the bold connections and parallels he draws without preamble—what the academics ironically refer to as assertions, could well be the report of a trail blazed by this idealized hypertext user, able to interact seemingly effortlessly with vast bodies of knowledge and experience. The leaps and bounds of his prose can be thought of as the very links and paths an erudite hypertextualist might forge were he plumbing an electronic archive of Western civilization from antiquity to the present for relevant inference. However, this possibility is as lost on the literary hypertextualists as the fact that the textual form is always, at any given time, a single surface because it arranges language for the eye. The only way to achieve the sort of simultaneous multiplanar compression that say, Deleuze and Guattari are reaching for when they introduce rhizomic or machinic assemblage as a key to their book *A Thousand Plateaus*, is to revert to the vast evocative spaces already present within the line of language itself, to stress degrees of fractural compression intrinsic to the arrangement of verbal information. This is what McLuhan resorts to when he says, "Symbolism discovered that in order to capture the live drama of speech you have to break up the sentence and break up language. . . . Symbolism attempted to capture a much larger portion of human speech and language."[48] The only means of presenting a complex series of jumps or links from thought-space to thought-space *in one frame-time* or *at one user interface* is to employ the resonant interval internal to language itself. Indeed, if one reads McLuhan extensively, one begins to notice that his prose is assembled with Flaubertian *souci* for *le mot juste*, so that it appears he is at every moment probing each word's semantic field, probing in the sense it has of *sounding*. Thus a single text surface can have screenal interactivity built into it insofar as it draws deeply upon the reservoir of language's verbal functionality. McLuhan himself referred to this technique as the presentation of "insights in a mosaic structure of seemingly unrelated and disproportioned sentences and aphorisms," as a "paratactic procedure of juxtaposing without connectives," and "the generating of insights by the method of 'interface,' " noting that "it is the natural form of conversation or dialogue rather than of written discourse."[49]

It would be, however, just as erroneous to suppose that McLuhan is interested in returning to orality, to modes of argumentation whose articulation mimics oral discursivity, as it is to imagine that language itself can provide the model for a hypermedium. Rather, McLuhan's thoroughness in looking at the alphabetic principle of the reading code as a purely technical, audio-visual problem shows textuality itself to be no more finally than a variable process of intercutting between two utterly distinct linguistic inputs. From this vantage, hypertext's preoccupation with interactivity is fundamentally a limit question about the combinatorics of two lines of communication in relation to the speed of access to thought: the line of visual sequencing and the line of spoken utterance. The question of hypermediatizing text, properly speaking, is one of maximizing the constructive interference of these two lines or data flows made available by phonetic technology ("Only the phonetic alphabet makes a break between eye and ear, between semantic meaning and visual code"[50]) so that the hypertextual drive toward recombinant textuality ultimately breaks down into the question of how much semantic meaning can be carried per line unit of phonetic visual code. Herein lies the clue to McLuhan's enduring fascination with Joyce's *Finnegans Wake* as the densest iteration on record. The microlexical slurring cum punning technique invented for this book is designed to attain the tightest possible synchromeshing of semantic meaning and visual code so that Joyce works almost seamlessly in the interstices of, as it were, heteroglyphs for the eye and homonyms for the ear. In terms of a textuality that has anything to do with the technology of phonetic literacy, the *Wake*'s fractal grammatology presents a limit case of language's hypertextualization, the hyper*text of* language.[51]

Below the threshold of this reading speed one finds all the forms and genres of literature that ever were; above this threshold there is only noise.

As McLuhan so well understands, Joyce is here applying the principles of the electronic tube or electrode to language and thereby to the whole history of culture and, as he alone seems to have been able to deduce, the message implicit in Joyce's invention is that the technics of phonetic literacy go right through language.[52] Electricity makes patent that the discursive continuum enacted by phonetic literacy's "complex shuttling of eye, ear and speech factors" is already driven by speeds of apperception far in excess of those language itself is capable of quantifying.[53] Where writing is a static, visual arrest of speech, oral sound is itself a freeze-frame sequence of mental motion, "a gesture towards externalizing an inner gesture of the mind."[54] Because with electricity language is no longer the fastest means of accessing and transmitting thought, it can no longer enjoy the privilege of conflation with consciousness, of depending on the long-standing entente which underwrote it as shorthand for consciousness itself. It is here that one perhaps best grasps the audacious economy of McLuhan's methodology and can see why, in a very real sense, his work eclipses much of the postmodern travail to come out of structural linguistics. For on these terms, the structuralist peregrination that marks the recourse to metalanguage reads as so many bonds issued to leverage a defunct expectation. The quest for a metalanguage is inflationary overcoding precisely because it floats on the projection that "there is always, on the level of language, something which is beyond consciousness."[55] As a purely local, terminological language problem, the post-*isms*' replay of the shock of modernity begins with psychoanalysis, with the great category mistake of the erection of the unconscious as a catchall annexed to language. That the unconscious is structured like a language only means that the very real *outside* and *beyond* of language can be ignored in favor of a parochial awareness no greater, finally, than the consciousness that language affords. In sharp contradistinction, language is for McLuhan a "technical extension of consciousness"[56] and a good index to the site of creative activity simply because it heretofore makes the broadest and deepest use of the senses. ("Language is the medium by which we undertake to convey experience completely and directly rather than as divided and refracted by a particular organ of perception; it may be less intense and precise than the various senses in their proper fields, but is deeper and broader than any one of them."[57]) As an "extension or uttering (outering) of all our senses at once,"[58] McLuhan's interest in language has therefore to do with the fact that its code group or significant unit is a *multisensorial artifact*. A word is a micromedium because it momentarily crystallizes an interplay between sense perceptions. Words are (multi)media events *in nuce* because each word encodes a unique distillation of sensory ratios, forming already a miniature closed system—as the task of translation belies: even between cognate languages, verbal transposition is only ever an encounter with the complex specificity of this fact that each culture is a discrete order of sensory preferences. The richness of the auditory imagination which is the template of language has much to do with the inner ear being the seat of equilibrium since the senses are in essence pressure, and pressure is the *sensus communis* or common ground of the senses. It is therefore "the hyperesthesia of oral and auditory cultures" that makes their psychodynamics so close a match for consciousness and explains language's huge bandwith of access to the pure stochastic processes of intellection:[59] "the content of speech is mental dance, nonverbal ESP."[60] So close is the working of language to that of consciousness that it literally required electricity to break the spell of their coextensivity. Where the "speed limit" of thought had once been set by the phoneme ("All the transactions in the nervous system involving language take place via the phoneme"[61]), the silicon synapses of electronic media shatter the barrier of phonological processing, introducing new *memes*, new ideogramic units such as pixels and bits capable of conveying experience not only as completely and directly as language, but with the intensity and precision of the various senses in their proper fields. Where once "audible speech split off from gesture and dance as a more explicit codification of interrelations," with the very microprocesses of these interrelations themselves now metabolizing the body and its codes, "today speech begins to look like an obsolete technology."[62]

In the question hypertext poses of language's relation to the world is therefore finally another one, a limit question regarding the relationship of the body to the world and particularly of the closeness

of its connections. Where hypermediacy is at base the drive to immediacy, to a kind of unmediated self-presence, the question becomes
one of the difference between mediate and immediate forms of
awareness. In the diremptive transition from a civilization of mechanism to one of electromagnetism that his diagnosis substantiates,
McLuhan works with an underlying physiological model positing
awareness as medially constituted, much in the sense Donna
Haraway intends when she observes that, "We are not immediately
present to ourselves. Self-knowledge requires a semiotic-material
technology linking meanings to bodies."[63] In McLuhan's acception,
this linking is performed by the central nervous system in the course
of transaction with the environment as a strategy for maintaining
equilibrium in the face of undue stresses and pressures. For
McLuhan, the question of self-presence is one of perception precisely because "what we take for our sense perception has to be fabri-
cated first."[64] Consciousness is the semiotic material out of which
bodies, like their extensions, are generated. We only ever apprehend
ourselves *in medias res*, via the perpetual perceptual mediation we
perform known as consciousness: "Our private senses are not closed
systems but are endlessly translated into each other in that experience which we call con-sciousness."[65] Consciousness is this (private)
consensus or *ratio* of the senses in dynamic interplay, orchestrated by
the central nervous system, "that electric network that coordinates
the various media of our senses."[66] At preelectric speeds, our
extended senses, tools, technologies remain separate, closed systems
in essence because they are always linked to the "mechanism" and
enclosure of the body, reliant in their articulation upon extensions of
this or that physical organ, and functioning in this respect as "fixed
charges" on the psychic life of individual and community alike.[67] No
need, in other words, of bionic prostheses to make the cyborg; we are
all already sensate cyborgs in merging with the products of our ingenuity as with "self-amputations" of ourselves, in the *re-membering* of
ourselves through what we behold. The first cyborg is, as McLuhan
points out, Narcissus. "He had adapted to his extension of himself
and had become a closed system."[68]

At electric speeds, however, the contour of the self exceeds the
outline and closure of the body as the hybrid mechanoelectric forms
of the mass media begin to extend elements of our sensorium at

speeds commensurate with those of dynamic interplay, clamoring as it were for collective consciousness, for a (public) consensus or conscience that makes *rational* coexistence possible: "media as extensions of our senses institute new ratios, not only among our private senses, but among themselves, when they interact among themselves."[69] The immediacy of hyper or electric media is therefore this fact that they bypass the intermediary of the body altogether in presenting us with what are essentially modular pieces of open systems, disincarnate fragments of our sensorial makeup or consciousness. At electric speeds, partial extensions of *sense-making* are also technologies of *self-making.* The open systems McLuhan describes with electric technology begin to make sense *of* us, to become part of our self consciousness because they deal directly in awareness and interplay as do our mental faculties and senses. "By putting our physical bodies inside our extended nervous systems, by means of electric media, we set up a dynamic by which all previous technologies that are mere extensions of hands and feet and teeth and bodily heat-controls—all such extensions of our bodies, including cities—will be translated into information systems."[70] Just how advanced this approach really is can be gotten from the fact that McLuhan already looks at intellection from the standpoint of virtual reality or proprioception, that is in the terms Jaron Lanier has in mind when he explains that, "Essentially, from a virtual reality perspective, the definition of the body is that part which you can move as fast as you think."[71] Dilation of the confines of the self beyond the integument of the body results from equipment of the private sensorium with phantom limbs which—in a reversal of the amputee's dilemma but with similar discomfort—each of us must strive to reincorporate as "technology pushes human awareness out into the environment."[72] We experience the electric feedback of our "techno-digested" disembodiment as a kind of spastic ballet in which all organs and functions, social and private, are coerced into interrelation at varying rates of speed and self-consciousness. The ideoplastic body, a body modeled by mental activity, is not a body without organs so much as a new "corpus" of exponential perceptual organs without a body, an amalgam of medial interfaces and simultaneous temporalities serving as "artificial extensions of sensory existence."[73] But these are only artificial with respect to the body, not with respect to (self-)identity. (The virtual body is only virtual with respect to the body proper.) What we feel as a simulation of immediacy or an effect of hyperreality is thus only a mutation in the scale of the imaginary, a loss of the homology between the self and those hypostases of the self such as body, memory, and language. To define the body as a "part" of thought is not to move the *products* of human knowledge or labor more quickly, but to dilate the very means and *processes* of human discourse and learning.

This is also why, finally, hypertext's equivocation with regard to the mobilization of language it proposes mirrors a confusion to be found at the core of an alphanumeric or digital basis for hypermedia. For if the concept of writing couched in Gutenberg's "twenty-six lead soldiers" appears to lead in an unbroken line toward the digital convergence of all analog structures,[74] there is the more pervasive determining factor that the theoretic and epistemological practice which letters realize—the definition of knowledge as a certain form of seeing—is at loggerheads with the forms and practices of knowing convened by electric technology. What begins in phonetic writing as a linear, segmental procedure for the visual extrapolation of information no longer possesses any of this homogeneous, sequential, repeatable and fixed character of organization and experience when it is accelerated to the speed of light. *Visual explicitness* is no longer the dominant metaphor for making sense, although now more than ever, it looks that way. With the availability of "the technology of writing by means of light itself,"[75] the continuum of visual, enclosed space built by Western technology's linear perspective yields to an unvisualizable, omnidirectional correlation of all the thought-spaces of the senses in their individual fields. That the new electronic space largely continues to escape the digitally minded indicates how literary hypertext as presently envisaged can completely overlook the global hypertext network long ago installed *in its users* by the delivery systems of the wire press. The omission may well be attributable to the fact that, as McLuhan notes, "It is very confusing to learn that the mosaic of a newspaper page is 'auditory' in basic structure. This, however, is only to say that any pattern in which the components co-exist without direct lineal hook-up or connection, creating a field of simultaneous relations, is auditory, even though some of its aspects can be seen."[76]

McLuhan's singular cognizance of this fact that information patterns assembled at the speed of light are in no way those shaped by the linearities of sight casts him as initial cartographer of cyberspace in fully describing the configuration of the new attention-structure, which he terms "auditory space" by way of analogy to the open field of simultaneous relations created by the act of hearing. ("Acoustic space is organic and integral, perceived through the simultaneous interplay of all the senses . . . the ear, unlike the eye, cannot be focused and is synaesthetic rather than analytical and linear."[77]) Specifically, he elaborates the dynamic of *tactual integration* that obtains within the spherical or total-field pattern electronically moved information assumes. McLuhan's work is in this regard a thorough exegesis of the state of attention Walter Benjamin refers to as "distraction" toward the end of his essay "The Work of Art in the Age of Its Technical Reproducibility." Typically one identifies with, and is distracted by, the general lament about loss of aura and therefore misses that which constitutes the enduring value of this essay, namely, the work on sense perception that prompts Benjamin to compare the laws of reception of film to those of architecture, finding both to involve an act of "tactile appropriation." This "new mode of participation" has, according to Benjamin, a "tactile quality," by which he means an in-depth, non-visual, haptic and kinetic involvement which promotes novel states of concentration and utterly different habits of mind.[78] Although Benjamin cannot see that, compared with television, film still carries an intense *imaginary*, he accurately foretells the evacuation of a specifically visual sense of detachment and authenticity. The power of the iconoscope (as television was first called) has therefore nothing to do with the visual resolution of the grid but rather with its opposite: the degradation of the visual to a point where the eye acts as paratactile hand in filling in the cool or low-definition image, inducing conditions of synesthesia that, as McLuhan puts it, make the viewer the screen. Passing through the vanishing point of representation, this tactile image exists in the non-di*visible* smooth space of any interface that allows its users to appropriate it "in a nuclear mode as a means of generating their own space."[79] In the quotidian cyberspace of "an electric environment of information coded not just in visual but in other sensory modes," one reasons by "the resonant interval of *touch* where there are no connections, but only interfaces."[80] If memory was once thought to be vicarious experience in which there is all the emotional value of actual experience, telesthesia (feeling at a distance) and tele-contact (touching at a distance) give us actual metaphysical bodies with which to experience real-time memory that—like *e-motion* itself—puts us in touch from within.[81]

In revisioning, then, the place of language as it impacts on the tasks of textual discursivity, and the possibility of text as a hypermedium, McLuhan's understanding is of language as but one physiological rectifier of the white noise over and against which media are what they are, now only one amidst many protocols for formatting data detectable in the random dispersion that is the continuous spread and flow of existence. When multiple pickups register and delineate the *textus* of consciousness at higher resolutions and with greater acumen, language is no longer that *fastest part* in relation to the speed of thought that lets naming appear synonymous with the active, independent, autonomous construction of meaning. Where language was "the first outering of the central nervous system,"[82] now there are others; as the partially-connected artificial intelligences of electronic mediation carve up the pure continuum of relativity, "we are all of us persons of divided and sub-divided sensibility through failure to recognize the multiple languages with which our world speaks to us."[83] While it is no longer the means by which our world speaks (to) us, language nevertheless retains a limited, specialized function as perceptual probe or "instrument of exploration and research."[84] It is McLuhan's prerogative to have seen that the type of discourse brought into being by the book is by no means the only form of discourse the book may carry. His *hypermedialization* of the book depends discursively on other media precisely as Deleuze and Guattari propose in adducing "no difference between what a book talks about and how it is made":

> We will not look for anything to understand in it. We will ask what it functions with, in connection with what other things it does or does not transmit intensities. . . . A book exists only through the outside and on the outside. A book itself is a little machine. . . . When one writes, the only question is which other machine the literary machine can be plugged into, must be plugged into in order to work.[85]

The authors are expressing acute awareness not only of the fact that "no medium has its meaning or existence alone, but only in constant interplay with other media" but also that, short of becoming "some quaint codification of reality," the literary form depends for its survival, or relevance, upon developing interconnections with other media, upon making contact with—in the sense of talking about—"the diverse and discontinuous life of forms" that are the media themselves.[86] Thus to continue to proclaim the book "an unparalleled medium for the delivery of high thought-content" precariously depends on it not being the *container* of thought-content at all,[87] but rather the locus of language's deployment as an anti- or counterenvironment, narrating in slow-motion playback a world that runs at frequencies and volumes far greater than those language devised.[88] For as McLuhan avers, "electric technology does not need words any more than the digital computer needs numbers."[89]

In this discussion of the import of McLuhan's work upon present concerns, I have focused on source problems involved in the transmission of his message. And here too I have restricted my remarks to a single thread of McLuhan's construction, the question of the linguistic materiality of the reading code and its possible mediality. Through the portal of these special, technical considerations of textuality's absolute material and physical limitations, the vast panorama of cultural effects and causes mapped by McLuhan awaits the careful reader. I leave the manifold tenets and discoveries of his research, and of its many fruitful points of intersection with the findings of others, to stand in this short space without commentary in order to mention briefly one final point.

This would have to do with locating the zero ground of an overall resistance to McLuhan's work, of comprehending, for example, the nescience with which academicians take umbrage with the spirit of the work as mock ecstatic or blithely optimistic. This sarcastic skepticism appears to have to do mostly with the fact that McLuhan's global village invokes Teilhard de Chardin's *noosphere*, with the idea that "with the arrival of electric technology, man extended, or set outside himself, a live model of the central nervous system itself."[90] Perhaps this has been off-putting for the same reasons that McLuhan identifies the environment as an "anxious object" and our age as one that endures "a total uneasiness, as of a man wearing his skull inside and his brain outside."[91] To locate this overall resistance would also be to account for this striking feature of the current relevance of McLuhan's analysis of electronic information structures, namely that his proleptic media fieldwork was completed with essentially nothing more than a tape-recorder, a little broadcast television, and some primeval vacuum tubes and computer "tape." The microchip's great proliferation of gadgets and networks, the laserdiscs and walkmen, the cell phones and pagers, video and cable and satellite viewing, multicasting and desktop publishing, work stations and think pads and chat rooms, telebanking and e-mail and other online services including global positioning for your car, as well as the larger conflicting sociopolitical trends of hyperdemocracy, such as separatism and balkanization in the face of corporate supranationalism—all of this atomization of communication that bears him out, McLuhan just missed living to see. Could there therefore be another medium that guides him in reasoning through the long-term contradictions of these cultural clinamina, while at the same time having become, almost by necessity, more or less invisible? While referring us to the fact that "the formative power in the media are the media themselves,"[92] *the medium is the message* is also pointedly a koan-like conundrum that asks what medium of communication there is that has no content, or conversely, how there can be pure message or information with no medium. And while the answer of course is electricity ("electricity is sheer information that, in actual practice, illuminates all it touches"[93]), one may detect a deeper allusion to the fact that the global praxis of relativity was instituted by the bomb. The idea that "electricity is in effect an extension of the nervous system as a kind of global membrane"[94] appears less strange when seen in relation to the phased-array radars that blanket the hemispheres in anticipation of incoming warheads, or to the nervelike constellation of wires encircling the Earth. Perhaps it is McLuhan's temerity at thinking through the full ramifications of atomic consciousness, of grasping the net results of nuclear communication, that still today keeps his work on the vanguard of information theory and media study. And if McLuhan works with a subterranean but palpable sense that the bomb lives inside our machines, that "World War III is a secret dimension inherent in our own technology"[95] and that nuclear consciousness is detonating and radiating throughout "the current *plasma* of superheated events,"[96] it is under this umbrella of total apprehension that he introduces "the role of the arts and sciences as Early Warning Systems in the social environment," where "art as a radar environment takes on the function of indispensable perceptual training," and education itself becomes "civil defense against media fall-out."[97] It is also under the aegis of this—for all senses—*ultima ratio* that McLuhan speaks of a "hyper-conscious culture,"[98] of the pending realization that "our environments are made of the highest levels of human consciousness."[99] Thus behind Gregory Bateson's remark that "in creative art man must experience himself—his total self—as a cybernetic model" lies McLuhan's preemptive exhortation to consider creative process as directive for survival: "Electronic man has to train his perceptions in relation to a total environment that includes all previous cultures. . . . The new possibility demands total understanding of the artistic function in society."[100] For McLuhan today there would no doubt be some significance in the fact that the Arpanet in which the Internet has its origins was expressly conceived by the military as a means of withstanding nuclear attack, of preserving operational command in the event of an atomic holocaust. It was therefore contrived as an interlinked series of distributed intelligences, of autonomous yet redundant brains, a neural net whose every remote node would be capable of reproducing the whole. In the cybernetic challenge to simulate consciousness, it may be a type of World Wide Web that downloads WW3, for here we find a mediate track to precipitate the program of absolute randomization, the (human?) alternative to autocommunication.

Introductory Note

1.   **Myth and Mass Media**, 13.
2.   Marshall McLuhan, *Understanding Media: The Extensions of Man* (Cambridge, MA: MIT, 1994), 8.
3.   Marshall McLuhan, *Counterblast*, design Harley Parker (New York: Harcourt, Brace & World, 1969), 31. See also Marshall McLuhan, "Preface to the Third Printing," in *Understanding Media: The Extensions of Man* (New York: McGraw-Hill, 1964), vii: " 'The medium is the message' means, in terms of the electronic age, that a totally new environment has been created. The 'content' of this new environment is the old mechanized environment of the industrial age. The new environment reprocesses the old one as radically as TV is reprocessing the film."
4.   The cover copy for *Time* 142, 22 (November 22, 1993) reads: "What Ever Happened to The Great American Job? The rules of the game have changed forever. Here are the new ones."
5.   **The Electronic Age**, 16–17.
6.   Marshall McLuhan, "Introduction," in Harold A. Innis, *The Bias of Communication* (Toronto: University of Toronto Press, 1951), viii.
7.   **The *Hot and Cool* Interview**, 69.
8.   Marshall McLuhan, *Counterblast*, op. cit., 111.

The Electronic Age—The Age of Implosion

1.   Teilhard de Chardin, *The Phenomenon of Man* (London: Wm. Collins), 240.
2.   Bernard J. Muller-Thym, "Social Effects of Automation," speech delivered to the International Chamber of Commerce in Paris, November 22, 1961.
3.   B. J. Muller-Thym, "Practices in General Management—New Directions for Organizational Practice," in *Fifty Years' Progress in Management, 1910–1960* (New York: American Society of Mechanical Engineers, 1960), 43.
4.   W. Heisenberg, *The Physicists's Conception of Nature* (London: Hutchinson, 1958).
5.   See Adolphe Jonas, *Irritation and Counter-irritation* (New York: Vantage Press, 1962).

6. J. Kenneth Galbraith, *The Liberal Hour* (Boston: Houghton Mifflin, 1960), 57–58.
7. B. J. Muller-Thym, "Practices in General Management . . .", 47.
8. ibid., 45.
9. Steven Runciman, *The Sicilian Vespers* (Harmondsworth: Pelican Books, 1960), 37.
10. Peter F. Drucker, *Landmarks of Tomorrow* (New York: Harper & Row, 1957), 96.
11. ibid., 97–98.
12. Robert Theobald, *The Challenge of Abundance* (New York: Clarkson N. Potter), 138.
13. Edward T. Hall, *The Silent Language* (New York: Doubleday, 1959).
14. Mark Schorer, *William Blake: The Politics of Vision* (New York: Vintage, 1959).
15. See H. M. McLuhan on "The Five-Sense Sensorium," in *The Canadian Architect* (June, 1961), 49.
16. Daniel Boorstin, *The Image* (New York: Atheneum, 1962), 4.
17. loc. cit.
18. ibid., 59.
19. Erik Barnouw, *Mass Communication* (New York: Rinehart, 1957), 11–12.
20. Gerard Piel, "Consumers of Abundance," The Center for the Study of Democratic Institutions, Santa Barbara, California, 1961. Single copies free.
21. Walter Millis, *A World Without War* (New York: Washington Square Press, 1961), 75.
22. William O. Douglas, ibid., 159.
23. ibid., 95.
24. A. N. Whitehead, *Science and the Modern World*, 141.

Culture Without Literacy

1. Albert Speer, German Armament Minister in 1942, in a speech at the Nuremburg trials, quoted in Hjalmar Schacht, *Account Settled*, London, 1949, 240.
2. J. Frazer, *Man, God and Immortality*, 1927, 318.
3. G. M. Young, *Victorian England*, 1944, 31.

McLuhan's Language for Awareness under Electronic Conditions

1. Lewis H. Lapham, "Introduction to the MIT Press Edition: The Eternal Now," in Marshall McLuhan, *Understanding Media: The Extensions of Man* (Cambridge, MA: MIT Press, 1994), xi; Tom Wolfe, "What If He Is Right?" in *The Pump House Gang* (New York: Bantam, 1969), 118.
2. Robert Everett-Green, "Marshall McLuhan. Resurrecting the Media Messiah," *The Globe and Mail* (Saturday, July 22, 1995) C1, C8.
3. See **The Hot and Cool Interview**, 70–1. Objection to the nonsequentiality of McLuhan's thought was, and continues to be, widespread. In a review of *Understanding Media* at the time of its publication, C. J. Fox, "Our Mass Communications," *The Commonweal* (October 16, 1964) 105–106, writes, for

example, that "the book swarms with non-sequiturs, terminological confusion, sweeping statements unbacked by any evidence and a usage of dozens of quotations that does violence to their authors' meaning and sets new records for tendentious reasoning." Thirty years later, Lewis Lapham, op. cit., xi, contends: "Despite its title, the book was never easy to understand. By turns brilliant and opaque, McLuhan's thought meets the specifications of the epistemology that he ascribes to the electronic media—nonlineal, repetitive, discontinuous, intuitive, proceeding by analogy instead of sequential argument."

4. Vannevar Bush, "As We May Think," *The Atlantic Monthly* 176 (July 1945) 101–8. In turning to "the real heart of the matter of selection," Bush notes that the human mind chiefly "operates by association. With one item in its grasp, it snaps instantly to the next that is suggested by the association of thoughts, in accordance with some intricate web of trails carried by the cells of the brain. . . . The speed of action, the intricacy of trails, the detail of mental pictures, is awe-inspiring beyond all else in nature."(106)

5. Gary Wolf, "The Curse of Xanadu: The Amazing Hacker Tragedy," *Wired* 3.06 (June 1995) 138.

6. Roland Barthes, *S/Z*, trans. Richard Miller (New York: Hill and Wang, 1974), 5–6.

7. George P. Landow, *Hypertext: The Convergence of Contemporary Critical Theory and Technology* (Baltimore: Johns Hopkins University Press, 1992), 3. Regarding networked realities, see also Benjamin Lee Whorf, "Language, Mind, and Reality," in *Language, Thought, and Reality: Selected Writings* (Cambridge, MA: MIT Press, 1964), 247–8: "It is the view that a noumenal world—a world of hyperspace, of higher dimensions—awaits discovery by all the sciences, which it will unite and unify, awaits discovery under its first aspect of a realm of *patterned relations*, inconceivably manifold and yet bearing a recognizable affinity to the rich and systematic organization of language, including *au fond* mathematics and music, which are ultimately of the same kindred as language." Emphasis in original.

8. The *Hot and Cool* Interview, 71; Robert D. Romanyshyn, "The Despotic Eye and Its Shadow: Media Image in the Age of Literacy," in *Modernity and The Hegemony of Vision*, ed. David Michael Levin (Berkeley: University of California Press; 1993), 340. Romanyshyn considers that, "Television as the shadow of the book makes visible the pathology of verbo-ocular-ego consciousness by challenging its values of linear rationality, contextual coherence, narrative continuity, focused concentration, infinite progress, individual privacy, productive efficiency, detached comprehensiveness, and neutral objectivity." (340)

9. **Myth and Mass Media**, 12.

10. **The Agenbite of Outwit**, 123.

11. Friedrich A. Kittler, *Discourse Networks 1800/1900*, trans. Michael Metteer with Chris Cullens (Stanford, CA: Stanford University Press, 1990). The quote is from Wlad Godzich, on the back cover.

12. Friedrich A. Kittler, "Gramophone, Film, Typewriter," trans. Dorothea von Mücke with Philippe L. Similon, *October* 41 (Summer 1987) 115.

13. ibid., 102.

14. Friedrich A. Kittler, *Discourse Networks*, op. cit., 117.

15. M. B. Griffin and S. M. Herrmann, "Technologies of Writing/Rewriting Technology: An Interview with Friedrich A. Kittler," unpublished translation by the authors. The interview originally appeared in *Auseinander* 1, 3 (Berlin, 1995).

16. Michel Foucault, *The Archaeology of Knowledge*, trans. A. M. Sheridan Smith (New York: Pantheon, 1972), 210.

17. Michel Foucault, *The Order of Things: An Archaeology of the Human Sciences* (New York: Vintage, 1970), 303.

18. **Myth and Mass Media**, 13.

19. Paul de Man, "Semiology and Rhetoric," in *Allegories of Reading: Figural Language in Rousseau, Nietzsche, Rilke, and Proust* (New Haven: Yale University Press, 1979), 9.

20. **Myth and Mass Media**, 8.

21. Plato, *The Republic*, Bk VII, 515d, trans. Allan Bloom (New York: Basic, 1968), 194.

22. **The Electronic Age**, 29; **Myth and Mass Media**, 12–13.

23. See George Landow, op. cit., 4.

24. Marshall McLuhan, *The Gutenberg Galaxy: The Making of Typographic Man* (Toronto: University of Toronto Press, 1962), 47. See also pp. 77–8, 124–5, 158.

25. William Gibson, *Neuromancer* (New York: Ace, 1984), 51, 55. In *Count Zero* (New York: Ace, 1987), 38–9, Gibson writes: "He'd used decks in school, toys that shuttled you through the infinite reaches of that space that wasn't space, mankind's unthinkably complex consensual hallucination, the matrix, cyberspace . . . data so dense you suffered sensory overload if you tried to apprehend more than the merest outline." Regarding the "romance of mass literacy" as unconscious process, Cynthia Ozick, "The Question of Our Speech: The Return to Aural Culture," in *Metaphor and Memory* (New York: Vintage, 1991), 165–6, writes: "The act of reading—the *work*, in fact, of the act of reading—appeared to complicate and intensify the most ordinary intelligence. The silent physiological translation of letters into sounds, the leaping eye encoding, the transmigration of blotches on a page into the story of, say, Dorothea Brooke, must surely count among the most intricate of · biological and transcendent designs . . . this electrifying webwork of eye and mind . . . . That specks on a paper can turn into tale or philosophy is as deep a marvel as alchemy or wizardry. A secret brush construes phantom portraits." Also in Cynthia Ozick, *A Cynthia Ozick Reader*, ed. Elaine M. Kauvar (Bloomington: Indiana University Press, 1996), 300–4.

26. Friedrich A. Kittler, *Discourse Networks*, op. cit., 109.

27. William Gibson, *Neuromancer*, op. cit., 170. Emphasis in original.

28. Marshall McLuhan, *The Gutenberg Galaxy*, op. cit., 1. Emphasis in original.

29. **Myth and Mass Media**, 10, 9. See also McLuhan, *The Gutenberg Galaxy*, op. cit., 158: "The printed word is an arrested moment of mental movement. To read print is to act both as movie projector and audience for a mental movie. The reader attains a strong feeling of participation in the total motions of a mind in the process of thinking. But is it not basically the printed word's 'still shot' that fosters a habit of mind which tackles all problems of movement and change in terms of the unmoved segment or section? . . . The print reader is subjected to a black and white flicker that is regular and even. Print presents

arrested moments of mental posture. This alternating flicker is also the very mode of projection of subjective doubt and peripheral groping."

30. See Paul Virilio, *The Art of the Motor*, trans. Julie Rose (Minneapolis: University of Minnesota Press, 1995), 140: "Speed is not a phenomenon, it is the relationship between phenomena. . . . The reality of information is entirely contained in the speed of its dissemination."

31. I borrow this distinction from Jerzy Grotowski who coins it as a means of marking the difference between the objectivity of ritual and that of performance. See Jerzy Grotowski, "From the Theatre Company to Art as Vehicle," in Thomas Richards, *At Work with Grotowski on Physical Actions* (London: Routledge, 1995), 122: "In a performance, the seat of the montage is in the perception of the spectator; in Art as vehicle, the seat of the montage is in the *doers*, in the artists who do."

32. Roland Barthes, *S/Z* (Paris: Éditions du Seuil, 1970), 10. Barthes argues this point further in his essay, "The Death of the Author," in *Image, Music, Text*, ed. & trans. Stephen Heath (New York: Noonday, 1988), 142–48. See also Michel Foucault, "What Is an Author?" in *Textual Strategies: Perspectives in Post-Structuralist Criticism*, ed. Josué V. Harari (Ithaca, NY: Cornell University Press, 1979), 141–60.

33. Theodor H. Nelson, *Literary Machines* (Swarthmore, PA: self-published, 1981), 0/2.

34. George Landow, op. cit., 7.

35. William R. Paulson, *The Noise of Culture: Literary Texts in a World of Information* (Ithaca, NY: Cornell University Press, 1988), 139.

36. Friedrich A. Kittler, *Discourse Networks*, op. cit., 111.

37. Critical Art Ensemble, *The Electronic Disturbance* (New York: Autonomedia, 1994), 95.

38. The *Hot and Cool* **Interview**, 60.

39. **The Agenbite of Outwit**, 122–3.

40. **Culture Without Literacy**, 128–9.

41. Marshall McLuhan, *The Gutenberg Galaxy*, op. cit., 138; **The Agenbite of Outwit**, 123.

42. **The End of the Work Ethic**, 100.

43. Michel Serres, *Hermes: Literature, Science, Philosophy*, ed. Josué V. Harari and David F. Bell (Baltimore: Johns Hopkins University Press), Chapter 8, "Mathematics and Philosophy: What Thales Saw . . ." 85–6, explains very clearly how the paradox of the increment rests on a quid pro quo of sight and touch: "Accessible, inaccessible, what does that mean? Near, distant; tangible, untouchable; possible or impossible transporting. Measurement, surveying, direct or immediate, are operations of application, in the sense that a metrics can be used in an applied science; in the sense that, most often, measurement is the essential element of application; but primarily in the sense of touch. Such and such a unit or such and such a ruler is applied to the object to be measured; it is placed on top of the object, it touches it. And this is done as often as is necessary. Immediate or direct measurement is possible or impossible as long as this placing is possible or is not. Hence, the inaccessible is that which I cannot touch, that toward which I cannot carry the ruler, that of which the unit cannot be applied. Some say that one must use a ruse of reason to go from practice to theory, to imagine a

substitute for those lengths my body cannot reach: the pyramids, the sun, the ship on the horizon, the far side of the river. In this sense, mathematics would be the path these ruses take. This amounts to underestimating the importance of practical activities. For in the final analysis the path in question consists in forsaking the sense of touch for that of sight, measurement by 'placing' for measurement by sighting. Here, to theorize is to see, a fact which the Greek language makes clear. Vision is tactile without contact."

44. **The Agenbite of Outwit**, 124.

45. Derrick de Kerckhove, *The Skin of Culture: Investigating the New Electronic Reality*, ed. Christopher Dewdney (Toronto: Somerville, 1995), 110. As de Kerckhove points out, this silence is a dilation of the complex abstraction by which we focus and "tune into" inner speech, filling the whole field of attention with an activity that requires tuning everything else out: "The reader is either in silence, or has made sufficient reservations in his or her mind to turn the ambient noise into silence. That kind of control, by the way, bears witness to the power of literacy over our hearing. When we read, we literally 'shut our ears' as if we had 'earlids' " (111). For a pithy discussion of the broader cultural implementation of this precise control, see Friedrich A. Kittler, "A Discourse on Discourse," *Stanford Literature Review* 3, 1 (Spring 1986) 157–166. The power of the reader to transmute random noise into a silence out of which he creates "the sense of a mind actively engaged in learning and in self-expression" is eloquently stated in Wallace Stevens' poem, "The House Was Quiet And The World Was Calm," in *The Collected Poems of Wallace Stevens* (New York: Knopf, 1954), 358–59. Here the quiet and the calm are that part of meaning and mind that assure "The access of perfection to the page," and truth itself is an absorption in "the conscious being of the book" to a point where "The words were spoken as if there was no book."

46. **Culture Without Literacy**, 132. Compare Ferdinand de Saussure's remark, *Course in General Linguistics*, ed. Charles Bally and Albert Sechehaye with Albert Riedlinger, trans. Roy Harris (La Salle, IL: Open Court, 1986), Chapter 6, "Representation of a Language by Writing," 25: "As much or even more importance is given to this representation of the vocal sign as to the vocal sign itself. It is rather as if people believed that in order to find out what a person looks like it is better to study his photograph than his face." The effect McLuhan accurately ascribes here to typography alone ("The discovery of printing gradually rendered illegible the faces of men" 131), Saussure erroneously assigns to all of writing. Precisely because Saussure doesn't *see* print, linguistics can become a general science.

47. Louis Forsdale, "Marshall McLuhan and The Rules of the Game," in *Marshall McLuhan: The Man and His Message*, ed. George Sanderson and Frank Macdonald (Golden, CO: Fulcrum, 1989), 170.

48. **The *Hot and Cool* Interview**, 60.

49. Marshall McLuhan, "Introduction," in Harold A. Innis, *The Bias of Communication* (Toronto: University of Toronto Press, 1951), vii–viii.

50. Marshall McLuhan, *The Gutenberg Galaxy*, op. cit., 27.

51. Eric McLuhan, in Barrington Nevitt with Maurice McLuhan, *Who Was Marshall McLuhan? Exploring a Mosaic of Impressions* (Toronto: Stoddart,

1995), 243, notes, "The *Wake* is a seismographic record of the perturbations of our senses, language, culture by our media." Terence McKenna, *Surfing on Finnegans Wake & Riding Range with Marshall McLuhan*, recorded at the Esalen Institute by Paul Herbert (New York: Mystic Fire Audio, 1995), says, "If *Ulysses* is the algebra of literature then *Finnegans Wake* is the partial differential equation. Most of us break down that algebra, few of us aspire to go on to the partial linear differential equation." Jacques Derrida, "Ulysses Gramophone: Hear Say Yes in Joyce," in *A Derrida Reader: Between the Blinds*, ed. Peggy Kamuf (New York: Columbia University Press, 1991), 579, speaking of the sequence of knowledge and narration "within *Ulysses*, to say nothing of *Finnegans Wake*," likens it to "a hypermnesic machine capable of storing an immense epic work, along with the memory of the West and virtually all the languages in the world *up to and including traces of the future*." Emphasis in original. McLuhan, "Space, Time and Poetry," *Explorations* 4 (February 1955) 62, dubs it "the ultimate whispering gallery of the human psyche, its vast nocturnal caverns reverberating with every sigh and gesture of the human mind and tongue since the beginning of time."

52. Notably, McLuhan locates the power of the electronic use of language not in the superdeictic visuality of conventional hypertext but in the resonant potentials of a transcriptional hyperaurality: "As a vacuum tube is used to shape and control vast reservoirs of electric power, the artist can manipulate the low current of casual words, rhythms, and resonances to evoke the primal harmonies of existence or recall the dead." ("Joyce, Mallarmé, and the Press," *Sewanee Review* 62, 1 [Winter 1954] 45. Reprinted in *Essential McLuhan*, ed. Eric McLuhan and Frank Zingrone [New York: Basic Books, 1995], 64) See also **Radio and TV vs. The Abced-Minded**, 83: "Now metaphor has always had the character of the cathode-anode circuit, and the human ear has always been a grid, mesh, or, as Joyce calls it in *Finnegans Wake*, Earwicker."

53. **Culture Without Literacy**, 128.

54. **Radio and TV vs. The Abced-Minded**, 84. See also: "Just as speech is a sort of stacatto stutter or static in the flow of thought, letters are a form of static or oral speech" (80); and **Myth and Mass Media**, 9: "For writing made it possible to card-catalogue all the individual postures of mind called the 'figures' of rhetoric."

55. Quoted in Fredric Jameson, *The Prison-House of Language: A Critical Account of Structuralism and Russian Formalism* (Princeton, NJ: Princeton University Press, 1972), 138.

56. Marshall McLuhan, *Understanding Media*, op. cit., 79.

57. Quoted in **Radio and TV vs. The Abced-Minded**, 81-2. See also Marshall McLuhan, *Understanding Media*, op. cit., 57: "Words are a kind of information retrieval that can range over the total environment and experience at high speed."

58. Marshall McLuhan, *Understanding Media*, op. cit., 80.

59. Marshall McLuhan, *The Gutenberg Galaxy*, op. cit., 27.

60. Marshall McLuhan, *Counterblast*, design Harley Parker (New York: Harcourt, Brace & World, 1969), 23.

61. Quoted in Bruce Fellman, "A Tale of Two Brains," *Yale* 58, 8 (Summer 1995) 44.

62. Marshall McLuhan, *Counterblast*, op. cit., 60, 117. With the automation of perception at electric speeds of simultaneous interprocess, McLuhan considers "natural and necessary a dialogue among cultures which is as intimate as private speech, yet dispensing entirely with speech. While bemoaning the decline of literacy and the obsolescence of the book, the literati have typically ignored the imminence of the decline in speech itself. The individual word, as a store of information and feeling, is already yielding to macroscopic gesticulation." (Marshall McLuhan and Quentin Fiore, *War and Peace in the Global Village*, produced by Jerome Agel [New York: Touchstone, 1989], 90–91)

63. Donna J. Haraway, *Simians, Cyborgs, and Women: The Reinvention of Nature* (New York: Routledge, 1991), Chapter Nine, "Situated Knowledges: The Science Question in Feminism and the Privilege of Partial Perspective," 192.

64. Friedrich A. Kittler, "Gramophone, Film, Typewriter," op. cit., 103.

65. Marshall McLuhan, *The Gutenberg Galaxy*, op. cit., 5. See also **The Agenbite of Outwit**, 122.

66. Marshall McLuhan, *Understanding Media*, op. cit., 43.

67. ibid., 21. Jean Baudrillard, "Clone Story," in *Simulacra and Simulation*, trans. Sheila Faria Glaser (Ann Arbor: University of Michigan Press, 1994), 100, puts it in the following terms: "As long as the prostheses of the old industrial golden age were mechanical, they still returned to the body in order to modify its image—conversely, they themselves were metabolized in the imaginary and this technological metabolism was also part of the image of the body."

68. ibid., 41. For a discussion of media as "autoamputative" functions, see Chapter 4, "The Gadget Lover: Narcissus as Narcosis," 41–47, where McLuhan advances the autoamputative power as a mediatory strategy resorted to by the body when the perceptual power cannot locate or avoid the cause of irritation: "In the physical stress of superstimulation of various kinds, the central nervous system acts to protect itself by a strategy of amputation or isolation of the offending organ, sense, or function. . . . The principle of self-amputation as an immediate relief of strain on the central nervous system applies very readily to the origin of the media of communication from speech to computer." (42–3)

69. ibid., 53. See also Marshall McLuhan, "Humpty Dumpty, Automation, and TV," *Varsity Graduate* 10, 4 (University of Toronto, May/Summer 1963), 27: "The electronic pressure to recognize and to follow the unbroken contours of the learning process is an inevitable expression of the fact that in electricity we have put outside us in an institutional and technological form those very characteristics of our private inner lives that constitute the unity of our private consciousness. The effect of electric information tends to create in the world at large a consensus of data which increasingly approximates the inclusive, unified field of private consciousness."

70. ibid., 57. McLuhan addresses the significance of disincarnation to the "human scale" and the paradoxical plight of the "no-body" ushered into being for all of us by the service environments of electric media in "Technology and the Human Dimension: Marshall McLuhan talks with Louis Forsdale," in *Marshall McLuhan: The Man and His Message*, op. cit., 12–24. See also *Who Was Marshall McLuhan?* op. cit., 44–5; and **The End of the Work Ethic**,

105: "In terms of the movement of information, it is the *sender* who is *sent.*"
Emphasis in original.

71. Jaron Lanier and Frank Biocca, "An Insider's View of the Future of Virtual Reality," *Journal of Communication* 42, 4 (Autumn 1992) 162.

72. The *Hot and Cool* Interview, 58.

73. Marshall McLuhan, *Counterblast*, op. cit., 116.

74. The letter or phoneme performs an artificial chopping up of language precisely because the principle implied in alphabetic abstraction is only nominally connected to speech, much as a technique is associated with its first area of application. In the atomization of human speech, in phonemic transformation's breaking up of meaningful sounds (speech) into meaningless sound "bytes" (letters), there is presupposed the very means of abstract ana-lysis itself, the disassembly of any process into *purely visual* units of one and only one fixed value, the alchemical extraction of sense or meaning from any matter or form via the "non-sense" of visual abstraction. Here, then, in the inarticulate subprogram of writing and print, in a technique that only the letters themselves stand for, is originary digitization, this parsing of sensory experience into visually abstract elements which have no directly sensible analogate. Letters are a kind of Turing machine for speech (they can "universally" simulate any utterance) in the same way that present-day Turing machines—computers—can specify the internal workings of any other machine and reproduce its behavior.

75. Marshall McLuhan, *Counterblast*, op. cit., 82.

76. The Agenbite of Outwit, 123.

77. Marshall McLuhan, "Marshall McLuhan—A Candid Conversation with the High Priest of Popcult and Metaphysician of Media," *Playboy* 16, 3 (March 1969) 59. Interviewer Eric Norden. Reprinted in *Essential McLuhan*, op. cit., 240.

78. Walter Benjamin, "Das Kunstwerk im Zeitalter seiner technischen Reproduzierbarkeit," in English as "The Work of Art in the Age of Mechanical Reproduction," in *Illuminations: Essays and Reflections*, ed. Hannah Arendt, trans. Harry Zohn (New York: Schocken, 1969), Section 15, 239–241. Benjamin also appears to anticipate McLuhan's view of art as a "contrived trap of the attention," as countervailing environment for bringing hidden grounds into conscious view, when he says: "Distraction as provided by art presents a covert control of the extent to which new tasks have become soluble by apperception." (240) See further Michel de Certeau, *The Practice of Everyday Life*, trans. Steven Rendall (Berkeley: University of California Press, 1984); and Margaret Morse, "An Ontology of Everyday Distraction: The Freeway, the Mall, and Television," in *Logics of Television: Essays in Cultural Criticism*, ed. Patricia Mellencamp (Bloomington: Indiana University Press, 1990), 193–221.

79. Myth and Mass Media, 11.

80. Marshall McLuhan and Quentin Fiore, *War and Peace in the Global Village*, op. cit., 7; The End of the Work Ethic, 100. Emphasis in original. See also The *Hot and Cool* Interview, 49.

81. Discussing the sensation dominant in virtual-reality cyberspaces, Derrick de Kerckhove, *The Skin of Culture*, op. cit., 43, observes, "Integration is a word that means at least two things. The first, everybody knows, is making whole

or putting things together in their proper way. . . . However, the word's much older meaning is related to the Latin *tangere*, which means 'to touch.' Not only that, it means specifically 'to touch from within'—its most interesting and relevant sense." Regarding the intimate role tactile extension plays now that speeds of interaction have increased to immediacy, he notes further that, "Tactility is involved with thought whether in our minds or in our machines, as a participant in the thinking process." See also Jacques Derrida, "Télépathie," in *Psyché: Inventions de l'autre* (Paris: Éditions Galilée, 1987), 247: "Oui, toucher, parfois je pense que la pensée avant de 'voir' ou d' 'entendre,' touche, y met les pattes, et que voir ou entendre revient à toucher à distance." Further corroboration is provided by Paul Virilio, "Red Alert in Cyberspace!" *Radical Philosophy* 74 (November/December 1995) 2: "Cyberspace is a new form of perspective. It is not simply the visual and auditory perspective that we know. It is a new perspective without a single precedent or reference: a *tactile perspective*. Seeing at a distance, hearing at a distance—such was the basis of visual and acoustic perspective. But touching at a distance, feeling at a distance, this shifts perspective into a field where it had never before applied: contact, electronic contact, tele-contact." (Emphasis in original); and by Jean Baudrillard, "On Seduction," in *Selected Writings*, ed. Mark Poster (Stanford: Stanford University Press, 1988), 156: "When the hierarchical organization of space that privileges the eye and vision, this perspective simulation—for it is merely a simulacrum—disintegrates, something else emerges; this we express as a kind of touch, for lack of a better term, a tactile hyperpresence of things, 'as if we could grasp them.' But this tactile fantasy has nothing to do with our sense of touch: it is a metaphor for 'seizure,' the annihilation of the scene and space of representation."

82.   Marshall McLuhan, *Counterblast*, op. cit., 42.
83.   **Culture Without Literacy**, 134.
84.   **The Relation of Environment to Anti-Environment**, 114.
85.   Gilles Deleuze, Félix Guattari, *A Thousand Plateaus: Capitalism and Schizophrenia*, trans. Brian Massumi (Minneapolis: University of Minnesota Press, 1987), 4. Also in Deleuze and Guattari, *On The Line*, trans. John Johnston (New York: Semiotext(e), 1983), 3–4. Testimony as to the resounding presence of nonliterary machines in McLuhan's writing is provided by one of the original editors of *Understanding Media* who noted in consternation that "seventy-five percent of [McLuhan's] material is new. A successful book cannot venture to be more than ten percent new." (McLuhan, *Understanding Media*, op. cit., 4)
86.   Marshall McLuhan, *Understanding Media*, op. cit., 26; **Myth and Mass Media**, 12; *Understanding Media*, 19.
87.   From copy explaining why HardWired, the magazine's new book division, was created. (*Wired* 4.09 [September 1996] 33)
88.   Noting that, "Print would seem to have lost much of its monopoly as a channel of information, but has acquired new interest as a tool in the training of perception," McLuhan adjudges: "Until the book is seen as a very specialized form of art and technology we cannot today get our bearings among the new arts and the new media." (*Counterblast*, op. cit., 99, 93) See also Friedrich A. Kittler, *Grammophon, Film, Typewriter* (Berlin: Brinkmann & Bose, 1986), 3–4: "Medien bestimmen unsere Lage, die (trotzdem oder

deshalb) eine Beschreibung verdient. . . . In dieser Lage bleiben nur
Rückblicke und das heißt Erzählungen. Wie es dazu kam, was in keinem Buch
mehr steht, ist für Bücher gerade noch aufzuschreiben."

89. Marshall McLuhan, *Understanding Media*, op. cit., 80. See also *Essential McLuhan*, op. cit., 261.

90. Marshall McLuhan, *Understanding Media*, op. cit., 43. See also **The Electronic Age**, 17, 35; and Jennifer Cobb Kreisberg, "A Globe, Clothing Itself with a Brain," Electrosphere section, *Wired* 3.06 (June 1995) 108–13.

91. **The Relation of Environment to Anti-Environment**, 113; **The Agenbite of Outwit**, 121.

92. Marshall McLuhan, *Understanding Media*, op. cit., 21.

93. ibid., 351.

94. Marshall McLuhan, "Introduction," in Harold A. Innis, *The Bias of Communication*, op. cit., xiv.

95. Marshall McLuhan and Barrington Nevitt, *Take Today: The Executive as Dropout* (New York: Harcourt Brace Jovanovich, 1972), 153.

96. **The Electronic Age**, 29. Emphasis in original.

97. **The Relation of Environment to Anti-Environment,** 113; Marshall McLuhan, "Preface to the Third Printing," in *Understanding Media: The Extensions of Man* (New York: McGraw-Hill, 1964), x; Marshall McLuhan, "The Care and Feeding of Communication Innovation," Conference on *8mm Sound Film and Education*, Dinner Speech, Teacher's College, Columbia University, November 8, 1961, unpublished lecture manuscript. See also *Understanding Media*, op. cit., 195; and **Notes on Burroughs**, 90: "We live science fiction. The bomb is our environment. The bomb is of higher learning all compact, the extension division of the university."

98. Derrick de Kerckhove, "On Nuclear Communication," *Diacritics* (Summer 1984) 80. De Kerckhove esteems "the bomb is right now the first truly active principle for the creation of a planetary consciousness. The bomb is the first medium to catch us aware." (80)

99. **The *Hot and Cool* Interview**, 58. Of humanities researchers today working in this vein of McLuhan's overall scope and direction, see especially Paul Virilio's studies of telematics as "pure war" in the genesis of "the world of virtual reality, that other world made necessary by the delivery speed of nuclear weapons" (*The Art of the Motor*, op. cit., 137); and Jean Baudrillard's analysis of an implosive, cooling trend in hypermedia and hypermarkets alike: "TV and nuclear power are of the same kind: behind the 'hot' and negentropic concepts of energy and information, they have the same dissuasive force as cold systems. TV is also a nuclear, chain-reactive process, but implosive: it cools and neutralizes the meaning and energy of events. Thus, behind the presumed risk of explosion, that is, of hot catastrophe, the nuclear conceals a long, cold catastrophe—the universalization of a system of disuasion, of deterrence." (Jean Baudrillard, *The Evil Demon of Images*, first Mari Kuttna Memorial Lecture [Sydney: Power Institute, 1987], 19. Also in *Simulacra and Simulation*, op. cit., 53)

100. Gregory Bateson, "Conscious Purpose versus Nature," in *Steps to an Ecology of Mind: Collected Essays in Anthropology, Psychiatry, Evolution, and Epistemology* (San Francisco: Chandler, 1972), 444; Marshall McLuhan and Harley Parker, *Through the Vanishing Point: Space in Poetry and Painting*, World Perspectives series, vol. 37, ed. Ruth Nanda Anshen (New York: Harper & Row, 1968), 7.

Considering the field of knowledge as a process, David Bohm, *Wholeness and the Implicate Order* (London: Ark, 1983), 63, indicates that "thought with totality as its content has to be considered as an art form, like poetry, whose function is primarily to give rise to a new perception, rather than to communicate reflective knowledge of 'how everything is.' "

Notes to Illustrations

a. Marshall McLuhan, *Understanding Media*, op. cit., 318.
b. Marshall McLuhan, *Counterblast*, op. cit., 23.
c. Marshall McLuhan, *Understanding Media*, op. cit., 8; **The Relation of Environment to Anti-Environment**, 119.
d. Marshall McLuhan, *Counterblast*, op. cit., 122; Robert D. Kaplan, "Fort Leavenworth and the Eclipse of Nationhood," *Atlantic Monthly* 278, 3 (September 1996) 81.

The original sources of the essays published in this collection are (chronologically) as follows:

"Culture Without Literacy": *Explorations: Studies in Culture and Communication* 1 (University of Toronto, December 1953) 117–27.

"Acoustic Space": *Explorations in Communication: An Anthology*, ed. Edmund Carpenter and Marshall McLuhan (Boston: Beacon, 1960), 65–70. An earlier version appears in *Explorations: Studies in Culture and Communication* 4 (February 1955) 15–20.

"Radio and TV vs. The Abced-Minded": *Explorations: Studies in Culture and Communication* 5 (June 1955) 12–18.

"Myth and Mass Media": *Daedalus: The Journal of the American Academy of Arts and Sciences* 88, 2 (Spring 1959) 339–348. Reprinted in *Myth and Mythmaking*, ed. Henry A. Murray (New York: George Braziller, 1960), 288–99.

"The Electronic Age—The Age of Implosion": *Mass Media in Canada*, ed. John A. Irving (Toronto: Ryerson Press, 1962), 177–205.

"The Agenbite of Outwit": *Location* 1, 1 (Spring 1963) 41–44.

"Notes on Burroughs": *Nation* 199 (December 28, 1964) 517–19.

"The Relation of Environment to Anti-Environment": *University of Windsor Review* 11, 1 (Fall 1966) 1–10. Reprinted in *The Human Dialogue*, ed. Floyd Matson and Ashley Montagu (New York: Macmillian, 1967), 1–10.

"The *Hot and Cool* Interview": *McLuhan: Hot and Cool. A Critical Symposium*, ed. Gerald Emanuel Stearn (New York: Dial, 1967), 266–302. The interview was originally published in *Encounter* (June 1967).

"The End of the Work Ethic": Address to The Empire Club, Toronto, November 16, 1972, in *The Empire Club of Canada: Addresses 1972–1973* (Toronto: Empire Club Foundation, 1973), 105–125.